EMOTIONS:
Mystery or Madness

Robert John McAllister. M.D., Ph.D.

Bloomington, IN  Milton Keynes, UK

authorHOUSE®

AuthorHouse™
1663 Liberty Drive, Suite 200
Bloomington, IN 47403
www.authorhouse.com
Phone: 1-800-839-8640

AuthorHouse™ UK Ltd.
500 Avebury Boulevard
Central Milton Keynes, MK9 2BE
www.authorhouse.co.uk
Phone: 08001974150

First published by AuthorHouse 1/30/2007

ISBN: 978-1-4259-8244-7 (sc)

Library of Congress Control Number: 2006911298

Printed in the United States of America
Bloomington, Indiana

This book is printed on acid-free paper.

FOR JANE

Who composes the music of my life

Note to the reader:

Names, dates, locations, and other identifying characteristics mentioned in this book have been modified to protect the privacy of individuals.

Acknowledgments:

My sincere gratitude to Joseph Heim, M.M. for his excellent suggestions and untiring diligence in serving as a reader.

I am especially indebted to my wife, Jane, for hours spent in valuable discussions, insightful comments, unending encouragement, and careful reading of the text. 1/11/2007

Table of Contents

INTRODUCTION

It is a challenge to write a book about emotions, knowing that it might be considered "just another book" on the subject. A recent check of Amazon.com indicated over 228,000 titles listed on the topic. Such numbers could be discouraging, but they have not been. There are a number of reasons that have prompted me to go forward with this book. First, the number of books already written indicates a tremendous interest in the subject matter. Second, this volume is not "just another book" about emotions. It is a work that carefully and thoughtfully looks at highlights of affective life in children, adolescents, adults, and the elderly. It will provide an opportunity to see significant segments of life from an inside perspective and learn from case examples how the same feelings affect the behaviors of each age group. Thirdly, this is not a self-help book but an informational book. It is not filled with formulas to solve people's problems, but it does contain information that can help them arrive at answers that best meet their needs. Fourthly, my experience tells me to write it.

I have spent 50 years in the field of mental health, obtaining a Ph.D. in Psychology and, later, an M.D., specializing in Psychiatry. This field provides a wonderful opportunity to serve people who are troubled by their past, conflicted by their present, or concerned about their future. I have had experience in a variety of settings including mental health clinics, private psychiatric hospitals, state hospitals, a state prison, rehabilitation centers, and private practice. Fellow workers have included other psychiatrists, nurses, psychologists, social workers, pastoral counselors, and psychiatric aides. The last four groups, I have taught and supervised. Encounters with all of these professionals have impressed me with the quality of most individuals who choose to work in this area and the excellence of care that is their standard.

Working with hundreds of patients who have been under my care has filled my professional life with gratitude and deep satisfaction. I have learned much in my formal education, and I have learned more from psychiatrists such as Frank Braceland, Judd Marmor, Chet Pierce, Dana Farnsworth, Howard Rome, and Leo Bartemeir, to name a few of those with whom I have had the good fortune to spend quality time. Most of all, I have learned from those troubled persons who have come to me for help. From them I learned the breadth and depth of childhood hurt, the uncertainty and fragility of teenage years, the struggle and turmoil of adult years, and the loneliness and apprehension of later years.

I will not claim any wisdom resulting from this experience, but I can claim a modicum of ideas and beliefs that I now feel a need to put into print with the hope that they will be of value to others. This volume will provide extensive and useful information for average persons who may want to know more about how their own emotions influence their lives and also how other people are affected by emotions. Parents and teachers will find helpful insights into understanding children as they obtain glimpses of how the child views the world. All those who come into contact with teenagers will benefit from carefully looking at "doubting teens" whose persistent question is "What do you see when you look at me?" Adults will find information relating to feelings about which they are reluctant to ask because the questions are too revealing of a lack of confidence in themselves and in others. Adults can also profitably review the tempest of their earlier years and obtain a different perspective on the onset of old age. Elderly persons will be able to review those childhood and adolescent years that shaped their adult life and come to a peaceful resolution of past struggles. They can gain strength and comfort from acceptance of the force that emotions played in their destiny and that must now be integrated into their elder years.

While writing this book I have had all of these age groups in mind. But more importantly for me the primary inspiration for the book has come from students over the past 35 years who have expressed appreciation for particular insights in discussing cases, regard for the manner in which I approached therapy, and respect for the obvious satisfaction I had in being a therapist. They found some of the case studies especially meaningful. I have also had a particular interest in the area of religion and psychiatry which will be obvious to the reader. As a result of this, the work will be of value to students as well as professionals in both the mental health field and the area of religion.

Obviously a book about feelings cannot be all-inclusive for such a work would take several volumes. The purpose of this work is, first of all, to reduce the mystery that seems to encompass our affective life and, secondly, to address the fears that are aroused when the subject of mental illness is mentioned. I have tried to meet these goals by considering a limited number of emotions which, in my judgment, are the more significant and prominent affective components in each age group. These chapters will include discussions, examples, and often case histories of love, anger, fear, sadness, depression, and anxiety. This is a small number when we consider that one list of emotions I found named 58 different ones. I will write about attachment and bonding as part of love. I will also frequently refer to curiosity. In fact, you may find that it seems to dominate the text at times. The reason for its prominence will finally be explained in Chapter IV. It might be more accurate to say that I have named categories of emotions in these chapters because many different feelings can be subsumed under the six I have selected. As an example, depression surely includes boredom, disappointment, doubt, apathy, emptiness, frustration, loneliness, self-pity, and suffering. A list of eight or ten other feelings could also be included under any of the other five categories that I have chosen to write about here.

Most people are aware of powerful forces that exist within, forces which can carry them to productive heights or plunge them into destructive depths. This awareness usually occurs when our feelings seem to take over our minds and control our behavior. "I was so in love, I couldn't think of anything or anyone but her." "My anger took over and I struck him." "I was so scared that I just ran and ran for blocks without stopping." "I felt so depressed that I couldn't answer the phone or the doorbell." "It felt like my heart was in my throat and I was unable to say a word." Emotions that strong get our attention! But emotions are with us all the time and affect our thinking, our sensory responses, our memories, our physical reactions, and our behavior. It is possible that people become uncomfortable when they reflect on the continued and subtle presence of this affective component. We cherish our decision making abilities, our judgment, and our self-determination. We have a tendency to believe that "being emotional" interferes with reason. In later chapters, we will address more thoroughly the importance and benefit of letting feelings participate in "making up our mind."

People seem to have little knowledge about how emotions occur and the impact they can have on our thinking and our actions. Rarely do individuals step back from their feelings and carefully consider how significantly their lives are being affected. Passions (emotions) may be transient or they may be lasting, but while they are present they are not likely to come under the scrutiny of reason. Depressed persons are unable to appreciate how their mood affects their behavior. Angry people are unable to appreciate their anger while their thoughts are tainted by rage. Anxious individuals do not realize how their judgment may be temporarily impaired. Unfortunately even after significant emotional episodes most people rarely take the opportunity to review the way in which feelings fueled their behavior. We may recall rather vividly our reactions resulting from our involvement in a disturbing situation, but we are unlikely to examine the "mood" that "drove" us into the experience. Some people try to hide their feelings; most people try to hide from their feelings.

Our first chapter will clarify the position that emotions have in our psychological life. This chapter is a rather didactic discussion of sensory phenomena, feelings, memory, reason, free will, and the spirit within us. I felt it was important to set the stage by defining and integrating the role of feelings in the "working mind." We will then proceed by devoting one chapter each to children, to adolescents, to adults, and to elders. As we expose and shed light on the psychological environment of each age group, we will include examples of affective reactions that are expected and commonly occur. We will also cite case histories portraying the influence of feelings on the lives of individuals.

Surveys of the general public reveal that by far the most dreaded illness is cancer. When we note the illnesses that are listed on the questionnaires that are used, emotional illness is never among them. If it were, I believe that it would be the most feared because it is the least understood. The common view of this illness is "being crazy," "losing your mind," "going mad." The ability to think and the power to control our behavior are two of our most valuable assets, although not always respected or treasured until there is the threat of their loss. Mental health care has markedly advanced in the past 50 or 60 years. The vast majority of patients are treated in office settings. Severe illnesses requiring hospitalization are less common and usually respond quickly to modern techniques. Chapters VI and VII will consider aspects of treatment with the presentation of case histories to illustrate positive benefits associated with mental health care. The final chapter will cover the relationship of religious beliefs and mental health treatment.

One of my textbooks in graduate psychology was by Dom Thomas Verner Moore entitled "The Driving Forces of Human Nature and Their Adjustment: An Introduction to the Psychology and the Psychopathology of Emotional Behavior and Volitional Control" (New York: Grune & Stratton, 1950). Not a very catchy title! I continue to be intrigued by the first part of it, "The Driving Forces of Human Nature." But now years later, I would modify it. Yes, emotions are forces that fuel our psyche, but we cannot allow them to do the driving. They give us the power to do things, to get somewhere in life, but it is the mental function of reflection and judgment that tells us which acts we should do and which we should avoid. It is the use of reason that must control the direction in which emotions take us.

This book became a goal based on my belief that people are looking more for an understanding of mental processes than for quick answers or cryptic slogans. I believe that most of us are quite capable of managing our own lives and making appropriate decisions, if we are encouraged to do so and given basic information about our own mental functioning. There is very little in popular psychological literature that encourages people to think for themselves or even to help them believe that they can think for themselves. Before the advent of talk shows and popular advice-givers, most people survived the cares and struggles of life.

Of course, life is more complex these days. However, the mind is not more complex. It has the same make-up that was present in our ancestors for centuries past. The mental processes that were used by people to write the classics, to construct the pyramids, to build the railroads, to cross the oceans, and to travel in space are the same mental activities we use daily in our lives. We should note that human minds also bring about war and other forms of violence and seem unable to solve the problems of poverty and hunger in the world. It is important to attend to our use of these psychic functions and our grave responsibility to apply them wisely and beneficially. In final analysis, the basic processes are the same and will continue to be the same. The "flat world" of Thomas Friedman, "The World is Flat" (Farrar, Strauss and Giroux, N.Y. 2005), will not change our mental functioning or our emotional reactions. We will have more information available, but will we be wiser and more prudent? We will have more material advantages in our lives, but will our spirits be enriched? We will have increasing contact with people throughout the world, but will our relational abilities improve?

CHAPTER I

Mind at Work

When people say "Make up your mind," they are suggesting that you make a decision. Rarely do we consider the complex factors that enter into the process of "making up one's mind." This chapter will consider the functional components that are involved and that may or may not come into play when we are in the process of making a decision. We will not review the expanding information that researchers are providing on the anatomy, neurochemistry, and neurobiology of the brain.

The mind is, in many ways, a processing center. It is the organ that receives information from the world outside, organizes the information, and prepares a response if needed. We rarely think of our mind as a processing center or an instrument. Our mind runs so smoothly and so easily that it is difficult even to consider examining how it works: how it gets information, processes information, and prepares responses, and how some of the checks and controls can influence our thinking. We marvel at the way in which computers can process, store, and retrieve information. Computer engineers are developing increasingly complex programs to provide, to store, and to recover more sophisticated and detailed information for computer users. Although scientists strive to obtain a comprehensive understanding of the mind, they find that its nerve pathways, cells, circulation, and chemistry are not easily understood or charted because it is a living, changing entity. The intricate and creative work of the mind is far beyond what any computer will ever achieve.

How do things get into our mind? Our sensory abilities of touch, taste, smell, sight, and hearing are the sources of direct and immediate input from our environment. Our five senses are the channels that provide what we might call "raw data" for our thought processes. Sensory acuity varies in people. These variations may be due to genetic factors, to training of the senses, to physical injury, to disease, to emotional state, or to the presence of substances within our bodies that affect our sensory responses. Just as natural intelligence varies in people so does acuity of the senses. Although people generally have the same range of sensory responses, there can be differences as a result of special circumstances. For example, mothers of very young infants sometimes appear to develop selective hearing ability. They may sleep through the siren of a passing fire truck but wake when their baby whimpers in the night. There is also the old story of the lighthouse keeper who trained himself to sleep through the regular throaty sound of the warning fog horn. One night when the horn failed to sound for the two a.m. signal, he awoke with a start and exclaimed, "What was that?"

I often wonder if some of the quarrels between friends or married couples may occur because of differences in sensory keenness. One hears something or sees something that the other one didn't hear or see in quite the same way, and an argument develops not because of differing opinions but because of different sensory input. Most people can recall having missed part of a conversation because they were not listening intently or for a moment their attention waned. They heard the conversation, but it didn't all register at the same level. A similar thing can happen with all of our sensory organs. Someone we know is looking at us and doesn't speak. We wonder why. Perhaps they were "looking through us," that is, looking in our direction but concentrating on some thought and not seeing us. It is not just hearing or seeing or touching, but it is also registering in the mind what we did hear, did see, or did touch.

We need to be conscious of the sensory input and able to process it meaningfully. What happens to many people when they are lost and ask for directions? "How do I get to the interstate going north?" The station attendant responds, "Take a left as you go out the driveway on your right. When you get to the first light, turn right again. Stay in the left lane and turn left after the second light. Then follow the signs to the interstate coming up on the right." Jackie Mason did well with this when he described the husband's remark to his wife as soon as they left the station after stopping for directions, "You thought *I* was listening! I thought **you** were listening!" Simple directions are never simple when you are already lost and feeling "not very bright." You hear what is said but it does not register in any understandable way.

There is another experience that many people have had. We sometimes see or hear something, but we are not conscious of it happening. Later due to some triggering influence, it becomes clear to us that we had a sensory experience which did not fully register at the time. Is it possible that such a thing happens far more often than we realize and that some of our best ideas were actually planted in our minds by something we saw or heard but were not aware of at the time? There is the possibility that I heard someone else express an idea which I did not attend to at the time. Later the same idea occurs to me, and when I mention it, someone suggests to my chagrin that I stole it from her or him.

The word "perception" must be clearly understood when people are talking about their perceptions. There are two very different meanings for the word. Perception can refer to sensory input, i.e., becoming aware of something through the senses. The word can also mean "a way of understanding something." In this meaning, memories and emotions and prior personal history become involved. Obviously this latter process is far more complex than the comparatively simple process of receiving sensory input.

Some examples may help clarify the distinction we are making in the above paragraph. Two women see an ambulance racing by with siren and horns blaring. They perceive the same event at a sensory level. One woman finds the event anxiety provoking and worrisome because her 16 year old son is having a driver's lesson at that same hour. The other woman experiences the event in a calm and unemotional way because she is a nurse and sees the ambulance as a rescue vehicle. On a Sunday morning two women leaving church after the service receive a casual embrace from the pastor. Both women receive the same standard embrace which the pastor reserves for women who stop to greet him. The tactile sensation is basically the same. One woman who recently lost her spouse experiences the embrace as comforting and supportive. The other woman who had been sexually abused as a child by her uncle experiences the embrace as invasive and objectionable.

Two men walking down the street hear a loud bang. They receive the same sensation. One man responds immediately with an intense alertness to his immediate surroundings because he is an off duty policeman. The other man responds calmly and has an inner sense of satisfaction because he is a car mechanic and has the thought that "someone's car may be in for repairs soon." A young couple sees their 14 year old daughter dressed in a new gown and putting final touches to her make-up as she waits for her date to take her to her first formal dance. One of the parents sees the daughter with happiness and pride because she is so beautiful, but with a tinge of sadness because this is another indication of her eventually leaving home. The other parent views the daughter with anxiety and apprehension because she seems so young and so vulnerable. They have the same sensory experience but a vastly different perception.

Many more examples could be given to demonstrate the manner in which people perceive the same event in very different ways. It is remarkable that couples and friends get along as well as they do since their perceptions of things must often vary. When two people are very close and have been together for long periods of time, they may come to a better understanding of the fact that the other person perceives things differently. This may well be an essential step to remaining friends or couples. If they tend to converse a great deal and if they are willing to reveal much of their past to their partners and if they are deeply sensitive, then they may even acquire some understanding of why the other person perceives things differently. One point is important to remember. No matter how long they have been together, no matter how much they know about each other, no matter how close they are, no matter how sensitive, they will never perceive events in exactly the same way. The price of individuality!

We have mentioned the five senses with which everyone is familiar. There is also the sense of kinesthesia which gives us an awareness of the position and movements of our bodies by means of what are called proprioceptors. These sensory organs are located in our muscles, tendons, and joints and act as a sort of global positioning system (GPS), telling us where our bodies are in respect to the world and where our various body parts are in respect to our whole body. Persons who are very conscious of their bodies probably rely heavily on input from their proprioceptors. Perhaps the best examples of the kinesthetic sense in action are fashion models because they appear so acutely aware of their bodies. Other individuals may also become keenly aware of their posture and their movements. Their kinesthetic sense may not be more acute but simply more important to them. They often appear to be assuming a pose. The absence of kinesthetic sensation caused by various illnesses can result in the inability to perceive and to control the direction or the extent of movements, a condition known as ataxia.

Finally, there are those who believe in extrasensory perception (ESP), the ability to receive information from outside ourselves without the use of our known sensory organs or at least the known function of our sensory organs. Thought transference implies receiving information from others without the use of known sensory channels. Clairvoyance involves knowing things about the present or about the future without normal sensory contact. While not adhering to ESP beliefs, many people are quite ready to believe in some sort of transmission of information that defies accepted sensory boundaries. They believe they have experienced times when they knew that something, usually bad, was going to happen or had happened to someone. Later they discovered that it did happen according to their premonition.

Patients have often told me of worrying about a loved one at a specific time and later finding out that something of major significance had happened to that person at that precise time. That sort of thing is not an uncommon story. Can it be explained? Perhaps it cannot. However, if we worry often about someone we love and then something major does happen to that person, we are quick to associate the time of the incident with the time of our concern. We need to ask ourselves how many times we worried in the same way, and nothing happened. Those times did not become significant in our mind so they were forgotten. Coincidence may be the explanation.

Lovers may be the first to claim some sort of extrasensory communication with one another. Two people can share so much of their thinking and their feeling that the resultant harmony becomes a pathway they share in many ways. They can certainly come to share each other's happiness and each other's emotional pain. In this kind of close relationship the heartache of one becomes heartache for the other. As a result, it can be difficult for one to support the other during a stressful period because the distress is shared so keenly by both. This is one of the reasons that chronic, debilitating illness or terminal illness in one person can be so overwhelming for the partner who feels called upon to be a resource. As a caregiver, he or she may suffer as much emotionally as the partner who is ill. Intimacy also has its price!

Memories of sensory information from the past are present in the mind and are often activated when a similar sensation enters the mind. Consequently sensory input from any source may be influenced by memories and thus take on a significance that is far beyond what the situation warrants. Everyone has experienced at one time or another how a simple sensation may suddenly trigger thoughts of other times, other places, other people. The touch of a slight breeze can take us back to the memory of a college campus. A melody can bring back a face from the past. An angry voice can take us back to a childhood incident. A sunset can recall a distant place from our youth. The mind is full of sensory information from the past, information that is often attached to significant people or associated with emotionally charged events.

Years ago I treated a young priest from Montana. He traveled from Butte on a regular basis to see me in Spokane, Washington. He had a recurring depression which became much worse in the winter months. The possibility of a diagnosis of Depressive Disorder with Seasonal Pattern was considered, but there seemed to be something else involved. It wasn't just the winter or the cold weather. Some short periods seemed to be much more trying than others. His history provided the clue to the recurring nature of these severely depressed episodes. He grew up in Butte and was the eldest of five children. His father worked in the Butte mines, and his mother was a homemaker. When he was 12, he came home from school one November afternoon to find an ambulance at his house. As he approached he saw the attendants putting his father into the ambulance. His father, age 43, died of a massive coronary on the way to the hospital.

The family was very religious. The mother and the five children, as an Irish custom, walked eight blocks to early morning Mass for 30 days after the father's funeral. It was a snowy winter, and there was often fresh snow on the ground. He remembered vividly the sound of the snow under his boots, that distinct crunching sound that comes from walking on cold dry snow. It was the sound that he would hear when making his priestly calls in the brittle white of the Montana winter. As he walked he would become morbidly depressed without making any conscious connection to his father's death. Fresh snow falls were the time of his worst depressive periods. The sound was just an auditory sensation in his ears, but in his mind it touched a terrible sadness of 30 years ago. Once he was aware of this particular stimulus for his depression, he could return to his father's death and mourn him again with the sadness and the love that is attached to such memories.

It is time to give some consideration to emotions themselves: where they come from, where they go, how they affect the thought process, how they impact the body. "Being emotional" often has a bad connotation. "Casey is a very emotional person!" This is usually said in a critical way and suggests that "Casey" is not an easy person with whom to associate. The important issue is not being emotional but whether or not the person's emotional response is appropriate to the situation. If a person breaks a fingernail and throws a tantrum as a result, one might consider the response overly emotional. If someone discovers that the new car has been stolen and responds by crying, swearing, and pacing the floor, the response might not be considered inappropriate. Patients frequently criticize themselves for being too emotional, usually because they have heard this so frequently from someone else. Teenagers may hear it from their parents, students from their teachers, wives from their husbands, and employees from their employers.

It is impossible to say in a particular situation how much emotional reaction is appropriate. The degree of response is not determined solely by the stimulus or by the circumstances. How emotional should one be about a loud noise? How much reaction should one show if one loses a wedding ring? How emotional should one be when told that her or his job has been eliminated? These are not reasonable questions. There is no answer other than to say that the person may need to show as much emotion as is genuinely felt.

A 25 year old man whose wife was shot by a drive-by shooter is likely to respond strongly to a loud noise. I once saw a 45 year old woman whose mother made her, at age 8, give all her toys away to "needy children." When she was 18, her father in a fit of rage threw away most of her belongings. She will probably always respond rather dramatically to the loss of things that would be insignificant to anyone else. A 50 year old person whose spouse has a terminal illness and who has five children, two in college and three still at home, is likely to be very emotional over the sudden loss of a job. You can safely make a judgment about the appropriateness of a person's emotional response when you have a clear understanding of everything in the individual's past life that may be pertinent to the present event. To summarize, it is rare that you can accurately state whether or not someone's reaction is disproportionate to a happening.

In addition to being affected by immediate circumstances and past memories, some people are by temperament more emotional than others. Temperament is described as an inborn tendency to react to one's environment in a certain way. Differences in temperament are recognizable very early in life. If you ever stood at the window of a hospital nursery, you may have witnessed differences in temperament. If an aid accidentally drops a metal pan on the floor, one baby may scream and fuss for several minutes, another may stretch and turn as if curious, and another may pay little attention. By temperament some people are more excitable, others more placid. By temperament some people are more outwardly focused, others more inwardly attentive. Persons who are more high-strung and externally occupied are more likely to respond with a greater display of emotion than those who are calmer and internally aware.

People may have different levels of emotional response at different times in their lives. It is well recognized that adolescents may be highly emotional. This will be considered further in later chapters. Some women report heightened emotional sensitivity during their menstrual cycle and menopause. Chronic illness may change a person's usual response to feelings. In addition, various medications can cause changes in emotional reactions. In mental health treatment settings persons who seem to be overly emotional are often classified by inexperienced clinicians as Borderline Personality Disorders. The latter issue will also be addressed in a later section.

As critical as we tend to be of people who are "too emotional," we easily forget that there are people who are lacking in emotional responses. These individuals are usually easy to deal with on a casual basis. They do not "rock the boat," and if the "ship sinks," they are not perturbed. They do not "make waves" nor are they disturbed by people who do. They respond in a reasonable manner to whatever happens. They are calm, but they are also bland.

Several years ago I had a neighbor who had this limitation. He never showed any genuine feelings. He went through the motions but not the emotions. A sense of gratitude was as close as he came to emotions and that was rarely expressed and then not with words but by giving gifts. In situations where others reacted with anger, he would make an intellectual evaluation and render a brief summary of the event. Circumstances calling for emotional reactions were considered from a more philosophical perspective. I still recall his reaction to the horror of the 9/11 tragedy. He was in New York City at the time. Later when he spoke of it, he seemed to regard it as a sort of historical event that he witnessed, without experiencing sadness or fear. He never showed anger toward his children, but he corrected them with lengthy lectures about their behavior, although he seemed to have no understanding of why they misbehaved. Thus, he separated himself from the kind of interaction with others that comes only at an emotional level.

It is extremely difficult for a person with normal emotional reactions to live with someone who is without emotional response. Major difficulties in communication are present when a hearing person who has not learned to sign has a partner who is deaf. However, the obstacles can be overcome in a variety of ways so that thoughts and emotional nuances can be communicated. With a partner who has little or no emotional awareness or repertoire, an important segment of relational communication is missing. Writing things down, sign language, lip reading, or any other device cannot bridge the void. The result is that the emotionally responsive partner lives the most meaningful part of life alone.

I saw a 46 year old male several years ago who came to see me at the insistence of his wife. He reported that she complained because he was not very communicative or affectionate. He readily acknowledged that he tended to "have little to say," and therapy established his honesty, at least in that regard. He was basically a "loner." He was reared on a farm in the Midwest by parents who stayed much to themselves except for Sunday church services. He had two older siblings who had both left home by the time he began high school. They rarely came home to visit, and he lost touch with them soon after the death of his mother which occurred five years before our meeting. His father was currently in a nearby nursing home where he visited him every few months. As a child he attended grade and high school in the nearby town but spent all of his free time on the farm helping his father. He remembered the names of most of his grade school classmates but did not remember any of them as his friends. He did not participate in any extracurricular activities. When he finished high school he went to college "because my parents thought I should go." Because of his interest in mathematics he decided to study accounting. He lived in a dormitory at the state college but had very little social life. He occasionally went to a movie with his roommate. After graduating he applied for a job with the Internal Revenue Service and was hired.

At age 32 he married a woman in her mid 20's. He had continued to attend the church of his childhood and met his wife there. She was a high school teacher. He described their relationship as good, although he acknowledged her dissatisfaction. They owned their home, and he spent a good bit of time fixing things around the house and making some improvements. Occasionally the two of them would participate in a project such as painting the house. He enjoyed the times when they worked side by side. Their only social activity was attending church together and going to some of the bible classes, with his wife's encouragement. His wife had friends from her work whom she would sometimes visit on weekends. He had no objection to the time she spent with them and seemed relieved that she did so.

I assumed that the two of them would at least spend vacation time together, and I must admit his response to this questioning made me suspicious initially. He took a two week vacation alone every year. She usually took her vacation with one of her relatives or with some of the women from work. During his vacation he would travel in the United States, visiting some place he had read about or going back to some city he had visited with his family when he was young. One year he traveled to Cheyenne, Wyoming to return to a restaurant where he had eaten with his parents the year he graduated from high school. He went there because "it was familiar." Sexual relations with his wife could hardly be considered intimacy and happened somewhat like the college idea. They occurred when "she thought we should." As I got to know him, I decided that life for him consisted of sensory input, perceptual appreciation, learning, memory, thought, and decision making, but no emotion or, if he experienced any, at least none that he could describe or display.

Comments about "being emotional" usually suggest that emotional responses are inappropriate or bad. Some people think that emotions interfere with a stable life. They fail to recognize that emotions are valuable sources of information about the world around us, and they are also the primary motivating force for much of what we do. I have often commented to patients that "emotions have a life of their own." They are, for the most part, a stimulus-response phenomenon. If you fall and break your leg, you feel pain. If someone kicks you in the shin, you feel pain and you also feel anger. Both feelings are there whether you want them or not, even though one is purely physical and the other is purely mental. If your stomach is empty and its meal time, you feel hungry. That is not by choice. If someone threatens you with a gun, you feel fear. That too is not by choice.

Emotions give us information about our surroundings and our situation. When we feel anxious or frightened, there is something real or believed to be real in our life that is threatening us. When we feel angry or defensive, there is something in our life that is hurtful whether it is real or imagined. When we feel affectionate or loving, we have discovered someone or something that stirs the response. When we feel sad, we have experienced the loss of something important, or we may only be anticipating the loss. All of these feelings indicate that "something" has happened in our environment and needs our consideration in order for us to decide what we should do about it. If we fail to give that "something" our attention and deliberation, then we could be accused of acting imprudently and impulsively. Paradoxically, we could be said to be acting emotionally, if we do not attend to those feelings that are present.

Having an emotional response is not the problem. That is automatic, natural, appropriate. Acting emotionally, which is responding without thinking, can be a problem. Emotions are like road signs providing information about what is ahead. Reckless drivers ignore road signs to their own detriment. If we have a sharp pain in our abdomen, we immediately begin to wonder if something is wrong, and we begin to review what an appropriate response might be. If we fall and hurt our leg so badly that we cannot walk, we think about taking measures to get it evaluated and treated. It is interesting that most people are quick to respond to physical symptoms coming from their body but are unwilling to value and reflect on information provided by their emotions.

Although emotions bring us pertinent messages, it is prudent to remember that the information provided by emotions is not always reliable. It must be evaluated with care and discernment. Then what good is emotional information if it cannot be trusted? It has merit because it gives us an indication of something that is positive or negative in our environment. It gives us a nudge or sometimes a shove. It's like someone who knows us well saying to us, "That looks good to me, or that looks dangerous to me, but you should decide for yourself which it is." On occasion, we get mixed messages because we are experiencing mixed feelings. If two road signs point us in different directions, it is time to stop and after sufficient investigation decide which way we really want to go. The teenager who has enjoyed the effects of marijuana can have mixed reactions to the next invitation to "smoke some weed." On the one hand, he likes the feeling it gives him, but, on the other hand, he is aware of the danger of getting caught as well as the possibility of becoming involved in serious drug use.

Not only do emotions provide information, they also provide the motivation and the impetus for us to respond. Anger can give us the push to retaliate or the strength to respond in a constructive manner to a hurtful situation. Some years ago I treated Charles, a 56 year old man who had come as close to losing everything as anyone I ever knew. His wife had left him three years earlier, and he spent tremendous sums of money in court battles to maintain joint custody of their four children. His business began to lose money through no fault of his, and he eventually had to file bankruptcy. While waiting six months for his pension to start, he was unable to pay court ordered child support. His wife arranged for him to be put in jail for several months. His accountant prepared erroneous tax returns and cheated him. He owed the IRS about $25,000. His physical health had deteriorated, and he was having frequent angina. His mother with whom he had been very close died six months earlier. He had developed an abrasive attitude which seemed to undo him every time he went into court. He was outspoken in the courtroom and could not contain his disdain for the female judge. It did seem clear that he had been mistreated before the law, and he showed me numerous documents that would support his claim of prejudice.

Anger seemed to be the prevalent emotion in this entire situation. A person would be terribly naïve to assume that judges are always impartial and only attend to the law and the facts of the case. Judges are not immune to feelings. It is safe to suppose that this particular judge's impartiality had been sorely contaminated by her reaction to Charles' hostility, which he had also been quite public about in letters to the press and to several political figures. It is not far fetched to believe that the judge may have used anger to retaliate against this man. His wife's wrath was obvious in her determination to have him incarcerated.

Charles' anger was a different story. I think it kept him alive, that and his love for his children. He often talked of suicide, but his anger kept him from giving up the fight in which he was engaged. Sometimes it is said that court battles can last a lifetime. This one well might. Anger is meant to be constructive, to be positive, to right wrongs. When I saw Charles for the last time before I left the area, he expressed gratitude for my care. I doubt that I had eased his pain or brought him better sleep or given him hope or saved him from despair. I had listened, and he knew I cared about him and about what was happening to him. Some patients unknowingly confront us with our own helplessness.

The history given above is an example of the powerful influence passions can have on behavior and how they can affect the course of people's lives. The daily paper is full of stories based on the results of emotional responses. Fear can be a force that enables us to flee or to cope with danger. Love is a strong motivating force in life that brings people to heights of tenderness, grand passion, and willing sacrifices. But when love is distorted, it can direct people to the abuse of others and to wrongful goals. The feeling of sadness is a response to loss or anticipated loss. It moves persons through the process of mourning as they experience the remembering and the letting go. Depression can result when sadness is not resolved. Later chapters will provide additional comments and examples of emotions at work.

We have looked at examples of exaggerated responses to feelings as well as the absence of such responsiveness. It is important to point out that there are all grades and shades between these two extremes. Variations in response depend on several factors. Genetic make-up, including temperament, is certainly an influence. Patterns set by significant adults in one's childhood also have an important impact. The experiences of formative years, as well as those of adult years, continue to influence affective expression.

Our incoming sensory information may be colored, distorted, enhanced, or obliterated when it comes into contact with emotions from the past. These alterations of sensory input can occur consciously or unconsciously, more frequently the latter. It is not only past emotional content that can alter our sensory perceptions. Our current feeling state also affects our ability to receive sensory input as well as our ability to interpret sensory input correctly. In later chapters we will consider various emotional states and how they can affect perceptions of our environment.

Although it is not the intent of this book to cover the neurological basis of our mind at work, there are two areas of the nervous system that should be mentioned because they interact frequently and often strongly with our psychic activities. The first of these is the sensory system of nerves which goes from most areas of the body to the brain and which carries pain sensation. These nerve pathways respond to outside pain-inducing stimuli such as touching a hot stove or being struck by an object. They also carry significant information about disorders or malfunctions within our bodies. Their messages of hurting can markedly affect our emotional responses as well as our thought processes. The mental effects can include worry, fear, irritability, sadness, desperation, and despondency. Physical pain can interfere with clear and logical thought and provoke rash decisions.

The other part of the nervous system that should be mentioned at this time is the autonomic nervous system. When teaching students, I usually associate the term "automatic" with this system because it is an involuntary system operating without our conscious control. It is composed of two physiologically distinct systems that are by-and-large antagonistic to each other. The autonomic system sends motor nerves to the internal organs, e.g., cardiac muscle, intestinal wall muscle, and other organs and glands. There are two components in the autonomic nervous system. One is the sympathetic system, and the other is the parasympathetic system. In very general terms, the sympathetic system is the system that prepares our bodies for strong physical reactions. Our heart rate increases and pumps more blood to our arms and legs rather than to our digestive tract, and the oxygen supply is thus increased in our extremities. Digestive processes slow or come to a halt. There is an increase of adrenalin in our system. Our body prepares for "fight or flight." The parasympathetic system is the system of rest and calm. Blood flow increases to the internal organs, digestion is enhanced, and heart rate is slowed.

Although the function of the autonomic nervous system is unconscious and involuntary, it is important to have some basic knowledge regarding its affect on the body. Imagine the activity of this system when a family is having dinner together, and everyone is quarreling. The sympathetic system and the parasympathetic system are at odds. Being angry stimulates the sympathetic system and causes changes as mentioned above including interference with digestion. But everyone is eating, and the expectation is that the food will be digested properly, requiring activity of the parasympathetic system. Is it any wonder if there are complaints of indigestion later in the evening? Is it surprising if the children develop "stomach problems" in such a household?

There is a reciprocal interaction between emotions and the sympathetic system. As a result, when the sympathetic system is activated by a strong emotion, the physiological changes will enhance the emotional reaction. Adrenalin is flowing, muscles are activated, the heart is racing. We are ready to go. It is easy to understand how anger or fear can escalate rapidly under this feed-back response. Similarly when the parasympathetic system is dominate because of the individual's state of calm, there is less likelihood of rampaging emotions taking control.

We have discussed how sensory input and information from our emotional reactions come into our minds. Now we will move on to the processing of that information. What do we do with all of it? When we are awake, we are thinking constantly whether we are looking at a nature scene, working on a problem, considering yesterday's activities, planning today's, remembering an old grievance, or just daydreaming. The answer to "What were you thinking?" is never "Nothing." The answer may be "I don't want to tell you" or "It was just a lot of little things with no particular focus" or "I don't really remember." The latter is probably the accurate response when someone is daydreaming. Daydreamers are in a sort of reverie in which thought goes rambling on, but awareness is diminished. Being lost in thought likely occurs when input from our sense organs decreases enough so that it has no significant impact. Our mind is then free to wander and does so, if we do not focus it on a specific topic.

The mind is obviously a storehouse of information from the past and a receiver for all information within the immediate range of the sense organs. One of the obvious tasks confronting our mind is to focus on a specific area and then gather pertinent information. In the normal course of thought this process works so smoothly and so naturally that we are not aware of it. The routine decisions of the day happen almost automatically: what time to leave for work, what route to take, what tasks to start the day, what to have for lunch, and so on.

When we face major decisions we become more aware of the mechanics of the mind. Suppose we want to buy a new car. We consciously set about gathering information. We look more carefully at new cars on the road. We are more attentive to the commercials for cars. We now read articles about car performance, check Consumer Reports, check internet sources, and visit dealers. We may talk to friends and family about the decision. We may check with our banker and accountant. All of this is sensory input. There may also be a number of emotional issues hiding in the background. "Can I really afford a new car? Will I feel better about it, if I pay cash or buy it on time? What happens if things don't go well at work? I always bought used cars before; I think it's time I treated myself. What will my spouse think about the idea? Will my parents think I'm overspending?" These are all emotional issues and cannot be as easily resolved as the black and white of factual items presented by the senses. It is important to acknowledge the emotional questions in making the decision and to address them even if they are not all resolved. Some concerns may depend on an indefinite future, "What if things don't go well at work?" Some can be resolved, "What will my spouse think about the idea?" Some probably don't need to be resolved, "Will my parents think I'm overspending?"

The above example gives some idea of how the senses and the emotions enter into our decision making. We need to gather facts not in an endless gathering process but in an adequate manner proportionate to the importance of the decision. We need to attend to the emotional issues that may be entering into the decision. They include feelings about our current situation, feelings that may come from long ago, and feelings that we may anticipate as a result of the present decision. These emotional questions provide us with information about ourselves and about what we are contemplating. They should not be ignored nor need they all be resolved. We do need to decide whether we can resolve them, overcome them, or if need be, learn to live with them. If we believe we cannot learn to live with the ones that cannot be resolved or overcome, then we should consider delaying the decision until a more propitious time.

In the February 17, 2006 issue of Science there was a report from psychologists at the University of Amsterdam suggesting that conscious deliberation produces better decisions in simple matters and that complex decisions may benefit from unconscious processes or what they termed "deliberation without attention." The idea of "sleeping on it" or putting it aside for a while may be of value when we face some important decisions. I have often encouraged patients who are struggling with a decision to make a tentative one and then wait for a period of time and see what feelings they have about it. Their feelings frequently help confirm their decision.

The last few paragraphs referred to the process of thinking, reasoning, judging, deciding. This is the ultimate function of the mind, the end point when sensory input, emotional reaction, and memory come together. It is at this level and in this process that we not only decide our behavior but also consider its appropriateness and its consequences. Our senses bring into our minds whatever they are exposed to. Our emotions respond in a stimulus-response manner. The initial control we have over sensation and emotion is to be selective about the stimuli that cause them to respond. In our present culture, there is very little evidence that people do much to avoid stimuli that may negatively impact their senses or their emotions. The secondary control we have over sensation and emotion is in our thought process and in how we decide to respond to what we have sensed or felt. Control and responsibility rest clearly at the level of thought and judgment.

All of these comments about decision making presume the presence of our free will. Occasionally patients complain about the difficulties they experience in the exercise of their decision-making ability. All of us, at times, wish we did not have to make some of the decisions we face. My comment to patients has been that free will seems to me to be one of God's greatest gifts. It is difficult to imagine humans without it. Each 24 hour period would be predetermined. There would be no decision necessary about when to get up or even whether to get up, no decision regarding what to wear, what time to leave the house, how to get to work, and so on and on, day after day. That would be the life of a robot, if indeed one could call it living. One might question what freedom there is for a person living in prison or what freedom there is for a person living in the grip of severe disability or severe poverty. In his book "Man's Search for Meaning" (Simon & Schuster, N.Y. 1959) Viktor Frankl wrote "To be sure, a human being is a finite being, and his freedom is restricted. It is not freedom from conditions, but freedom to take a stand toward the conditions." The harsh life of a concentration camp was part of the background for his statement.

Finally, in this chapter on components of the mind it is essential to introduce the concept of spirit or soul. Some readers may have difficulty with a reference to something spiritual as part of the mind. They probably conclude that spirit suggests a deity and life hereafter. It is true that if spirit is involved it cannot stand alone, for it must have some counterpart. There must be a source or a force which brings this spirit to the scene because it is not just a sensory phenomenon, not simply an emotional reaction, not the vestige of some memory, and not only a matter of judgment. Spirit cannot be the result of some conglomerate of nerve cells, for nerve cells can be damaged by the ravages of sickness, but spirit continues to survive. It is not destroyed by disease. It is not extinguished by experience. Indeed, it often becomes more prominent in adversity and more impressive in illness.

It has always been an inspiration to me to see people whose lives have, for a long time, gone from one tragedy to another, and their spirit remains their source of strength. They may not attend church. They may not do much formal praying. They may not talk much about God or eternity, but they clearly express a belief that there is more to their life than they see or can understand. They find some mystery in their hardships, and the mystery stirs some sense of a world that is beyond what they currently know. They are typically reluctant to try to describe these feelings, perhaps because they seem foreign, fragile, or uncertain. In "The Weight of Glory" (Eerdmans Publishing, Grand Rapids, MI, 1949), C.S. Lewis speaks of this as a desire for a "far-off country" and describes it as, "The secret we cannot hide and cannot tell, though we desire to do both. We cannot tell it because it is a desire for something that has never actually appeared in our experience. We cannot hide it because our experience is constantly suggesting it, and we betray ourselves like lovers at the mention of a name."

When I served as director of an adolescent inpatient program, we had regular morning team meetings to discuss new admissions and to review current patients. After some time working together, the idea of luncheon meetings was proposed so that we could talk about other things. At one of these meetings, the topic of religion came up for discussion. One of the social workers commented that she wished she could have some religious belief because she felt she had none. Since she knew I was Catholic, she asked me why I believed. Of course that could be a long story, but my answer was brief. I responded, "In the light of my experiences in life, I cannot not believe." I later teased her about her "faith" when she mentioned that in making telephone calls to one of her children she always had to say certain things to him before they hung up so that he would be safe from harm. On one occasion the connection was lost before she completed her ritual, and she was worried that some danger would befall him. It always seems to me that rituals are secret prayers to an unnamed God. Discussion regarding the interface of psychotherapy and religion will appear in the last chapter.

CHAPTER II

The Challenge of Childhood

The above title was not chosen to suggest that children are a challenge for their parents, although there is a great deal of truth in that thought. The title was chosen to emphasize the fact that childhood because of the breadth of its experiences, the pace of its learning curve, and the intensity and significance of its emotional reactions is indeed a challenge to the newborn. The child is constantly being tested by the environment, evaluated by adults, and judged by outside observers. The newborn does not realize that he or she has been born into a society of standards, a culture of comparisons, and an environment of expectations. The standards, comparisons, and expectations are transmitted from parent to child early in the parent-child relationship. The process is later continued by grandparents, other relatives, teachers, and neighbors. It seems that some persons live in the shadow of these criteria throughout their entire lives.

The primary premise of this book is that the majority of people are able to think things through for themselves, providing they have sufficient information about the subject. Another premise of the book is that in our interactions with other persons we are usually thinking about what our position is rather than what their position is. A prime example of this is the relationship of parent and child. Parents are concerned about their parenting skills and become very aware of what they are doing as parents. They focus on their ability to talk to the child, their attitudes regarding the child's behavior, their involvement in the child's activities, and their methods of discipline. All of this focuses on their view of themselves in relation to the child. It is appropriate for a parent to wonder "What kind of a parent am I?" However, that is looking at the parent-child dyad from the parent's perspective. Here let us try to look at the relationship from the child's point of view.

In teaching students who want to become therapists I have found that it is very difficult for them to stop focusing on what they are doing as counselors (their world) and to attend to what is happening in their client's world. The goal is not just to hear what is happening to the client but to understand how the client perceives and experiences what is happening. The counselor will know how to respond when he or she can perceive the world the way the client does. Once that happens, then a caring and empathic counselor will be able to respond to the person in a sensitive manner congruent with the need. Obviously the student must also learn a great deal about the principles of good therapy and have an adequate knowledge of the interactions that may occur in the counseling process. After those basics are acquired the therapeutic encounter is all about the client.

A similar approach is appropriate for those who are raising children. Certainly parents should have an adequate knowledge of their role as well as the needs of the children in the family. Some couples have had positive examples of attitudes and behaviors from their parents. Others have not had the benefit of observing good parenting in their own childhood. Raising a child is one of the most serious obligations that anyone can assume. Unfortunately it often comes about without any planning or preparation. All too frequently, young people who still need parenting themselves are becoming parents before they have achieved the fullness of their own adolescent development. Classes in child rearing are becoming more popular. Some churches encourage or even require instructions before marriage, and some offer classes for young mothers and fathers. Books which provide knowledge about fundamental skills for their role are worth while, but parents must remember that every child is unique and requires an adaptation of techniques.

To continue the comparison with novice counselors, parents are better able to respond to the child when they appreciate how the child sees the world. The goal of the remainder of this chapter is to give parents some understanding of the child's view of the world. In the previous chapter we considered how sensory input and emotional reactions take place. Here we will look at some of the sensory input children receive and some of their common reactions.

Researches tell us that all the sensory organs of the child are functioning soon after birth. Although the child sees and hears, tastes and feels and smells, the ability to determine the sources or the significance of these sensations is initially absent. As months and years pass and nerve pathways continue to develop, the child learns to differentiate faces, sounds, and other sensory stimuli. It is important for parents and others working with children to know that youngsters can experience sensory overload. Although their senses may be functioning, their ability to process the information they are receiving may be delayed or not clearly organized. The child may appear bewildered and unable to respond. If the adult then becomes impatient and irritated, the child's responsiveness will only deteriorate further.

Several years ago I saw a 10 year old boy whose mother stated that he had been diagnosed by a pediatrician as having severe Attention Deficit Disorder. At the time of my evaluation Joseph was taking Adderall, an appropriate medicine for the disorder. I continued him on the medicine pending additional interviews and the opportunity to know him better. Initially his mother insisted on staying in my office during each visit, though I told her that was not my policy or my recommendation. I had the impression that if I did not permit this for a few sessions they would not return for treatment.

During these initial meetings the mother did most of the talking, detailing the misbehavior of her son and his utter failure to respond to her directions at home. He was seemingly inattentive to her verbal onslaught and sat quietly except for some fidgeting with his hands or the sides of the chair. After several sessions I finally persuaded the mother to let me meet with Joseph alone. She would then accost me in the waiting room before or after the visit to pour out the problems she had encountered at home trying to deal with his inattention and his failure to complete anything he was asked to do. Because of time constraints I eventually asked her to write out these problems and give them to me at the beginning of each interview. She brought in two or three pages each week.

Meeting with Joseph by himself was quite a different experience. He was attentive, responsive to questions, and volunteered information about himself and his family. Concentration was good, and there was no evidence of distractibility. He was obtaining high average grades, and there were no complaints from teachers regarding his behavior. There was no conflict with neighbors, and from his report he had friends in the neighborhood and was welcome in their houses. His manner during interview was bright and engaging. He was, in fact, quite a different boy when he was seen without his mother. Joseph said that he got along well with his father, and his mother never indicated otherwise. I had the impression that his father was not his advocate in relation to the mother, perhaps because of her hyper-critical and somewhat aggressive manner. That may have been the price the father paid to keep the marriage intact.

When I made positive comments about Joseph to his mother at the end of interviews, it seemed to irritate her. I continued him on the same dosage of Adderall, although his mother regularly pressed for an increase in the medicine or a trial on an alternative stimulant. At one point I suggested that we try him without the medicine for two or three weeks and see how things went. She was adamantly opposed. I also suggested, as tactfully as I could, that it might be helpful if she and her husband would see a counselor "to help them deal more effectively" with their son. Soon after that she left a message canceling the next appointment and saying that they were taking Joseph somewhere else. It was hardly a surprise to me.

About 18 months later I received a brief letter stating that they were sending Joseph to a Wilderness Program and requesting that records be sent there. I do not believe this youngster had an Attention Deficit Disorder. I had continued his medication with the hope of reaching a point where I could convince his mother that medicine was not the answer and that some family counseling was. I believe that Joseph was not an oppositional boy, and there was plenty of evidence suggesting he was not. Nor do I believe that he was deliberately defiant of his mother. I think she came at him like a whirlwind with demands and criticisms and anger and a litany of his failures, all at one time, and Joseph's mental capabilities were overloaded. As a result, he could not process what she was saying and he became bewildered, unresponsive, and inattentive. I will refer to Wilderness Programs again in the chapter on treatment.

During the very early developmental period certain features of the child's world are obvious. The child is helpless and depends on others to respond to physical needs. It is also clear from infant behavior that the young child has emotional needs and responds to those who fulfill them. During the first year of life the child begins to identify the face and the voice of the mother as the principal caretaker and is able to signal for attention from the mother. Signaling is done by crying or by babbling sounds. Experiments have shown that cry prints are distinctive and can be identified by the mother. I grew up on a ranch in Montana and remember in the spring seeing cows, in a herd of two hundred or more, reunite with their calves, identified by their mooing. This early interaction between infant and mother continues when the child is able to walk and tries to follow mother wherever she goes.

Maintaining proximity to the mother provides the child with an initial sense of security. The child feels safe when the mother is in sight and later feels safe when the mother is not visible but available. The next step is for the child to accept the mother's absence and a substitute caretaker.

In today's culture, mothers are not always available to go through these natural stages. Someone else may be the primary caretaker, or there may be more than one caretaker involved. Nevertheless, it is important for parents to understand this developmental period which the child is experiencing. It is one of many that will occur. It is especially significant because this process is the foundation of the child's ability to attach to another person. After this initial attachment to the primary caretaker, the child becomes attached to inanimate objects: a cuddly toy, a blanket, a piece of clothing. Psychologists speak of these as transitional objects. Attachment to transitional objects may extend into early school years. The abrupt loss of one of these treasured items can be traumatic for a child and cause temporary regression marked by sadness, irritability, and increased demands for attention from mother. Attachment to other persons develops during this period. This ability to connect to others and to objects is essential for healthy maturation.

Parents who have adopted children from foreign countries where early care may have been grossly inadequate occasionally become concerned about the apparent inability of the children to make meaningful connections to the adoptive parents. There is a psychiatric disorder called Reactive Attachment Disorder of Infancy or Early Childhood which begins before the age of 5. The disorder is associated with early pathological care including failure to respond to the child's emotional needs for comfort, stimulation, and affection. Other causes include failure to respond to the child's basic physical needs or frequent changes in the primary caregiver.

This attachment disorder is characterized by failure to respond normally to social interactions or by engaging in diffuse and indiscriminate social attachments. There is considerable evidence suggesting that the development of the attachment response is an age specific behavior, which means that, if this ability to connect to others is not established during these formative years before age 5, the individual will not be able either to learn or to exhibit this response later in life.

Many adults say how baffled and confused they are by the electronic age in which we suddenly find ourselves. There is a great deal to learn, and it all seems to be in a foreign language. There are new words, and old words have new meanings. Imagine how much there is for young children to learn and how much information bombards them from all their sense organs. As they receive information from various sensory stimuli they are also keenly aware of the emotional setting of all that they see and hear. Young children are sensitive to the feelings exhibited by their caregivers.

When a parent and child are waiting in line in a store and the child begins to misbehave in some manner, we hear the parent say to the child, "Don't do that" or "Please stop that." The words may be repeated several times with the child paying little attention. The voice is soft and gentle, not much different than if the parent were saying, "You look nice today" or "We'll be leaving soon." The emotional tone is flat and does not fit the parent's annoyance or the corrective statement. The manner in which it is said carries no evidence that the parent expects the child to comply. It suggests to the bystander that this is a frequent exchange between this parent and child which is routinely dismissed by them both. However, if the bad behavior escalates or if the mother or father becomes impatient because of the long wait in line, the adult may suddenly become quite irritated with the child's conduct, pull the child roughly, and say very harshly and very loudly, "How many times have I told you to stop that?" The answer is really "None." The parent did not, during the earlier scene, get the child's full attention and say in a forceful manner with a stern but caring tone, "**Please, stop doing that**."

There are subtle cues given by people when they experience emotions such as anger or fear even though they may try to hide the feelings from others. We have all known a situation in which we were keenly aware that someone in the room was very angry although no one had indicated it directly. It is difficult to say how we knew it, other than to say we could "feel it in the air." We could easily state what the feeling was in the room and usually identify the source. Young children are limited verbally and would probably have difficulty being able to identify in words what they know someone else's feeling is. Perhaps because the young have no words for what they observe, the emotional state of a significant person may have even greater impact on them.

I have often asked patients who spoke of the force and frequency of parental anger, "How did you know that your parent was angry?" The answer was usually "I just knew it." Strong feelings are communicated to others. I am not suggesting that parents should not exhibit strong feelings around their children, but they need to be aware that their feelings are quickly detected by the children who can "feel it in the air." Certain emotions are contagious. Fearful and tense individuals stimulate anxious feelings in others who are around them. Children typically respond to episodes of parental anxiety, fear, or anger with apprehension of their own.

Several years ago a 28 year old single woman came to see me because of severe anxiety and insomnia. She had obtained some benefit from tranquilizers and sedatives, but those were obviously not a long term solution for her. In the discussion of her early life she reported that when she was 3 or 4 years old she and her younger sister would often be awakened in the night by their mother and taken into the mother's bed. Their father worked very late at night in a dangerous area of town, and his work necessitated carrying large sums of money. He was expected home shortly after midnight but often did not return until 2 or 3 AM. The mother either did not get to sleep, or if she did, she would invariably awaken around midnight expecting him home. As her anxiety increased after midnight, she woke her daughters to be with her and distract her from her frightening thoughts. As one might expect, her anxiety was quickly transmitted to her children, and all three worried and wept until the father came home.

My patient remembered how her anxiety of the night soon spread into the daylight hours and began to include worrying about her sister and her mother. Before long, when anyone left the house, she was terrified by the thought that the person would not return. Eventually she worried that the other family members would all die, and she would be left alone. Anxiety became part of her everyday life and was increasingly debilitating for her as she faced the challenges of adulthood and the threat of her parents' aging and poor health. With continued therapy she became more confident of her own abilities and better able to face the uncertainties of the future, resulting in improved sleep and improved control of her anxious patterns of thought.

It is difficult to distinguish between anxiety and fear in children as well as in adults. Anxiety is used to describe situations in which a person exhibits apprehension, worry, or tension due to a definite cause or when a person reports these same feelings but without an apparent reason. If a person is called upon to speak in front of a group of people, anxiety typically occurs. Some people are uneasy when they go to their doctor even for a regular check-up. Most people have experienced a time when they had a sense of foreboding or concern without being able to say why. We speak of fear when there is a situation which carries a potential threat of harm. If we think there is a prowler outside our house, we are likely to feel frightened because danger is assumed to be present. When we discover it's the neighbor coming to borrow the lawn mower, our fear is gone. If we are scheduled for an operation, we may be fearful because risks are involved. Of course, when the surgeon goes through the list of possible complications including death, our fear is not allayed. "Informed consent" rarely soothes one's nerves, but a good surgeon can. Fear and anxiety are generally used interchangeably, and we will use them in that manner unless we clearly indicate otherwise.

Children have difficulty distinguishing between something that is only frightening and something that is dangerous. A baby may scream when picked up by the grandmother. Everyone hastens to explain, "The baby is afraid of you, because you're wearing glasses." We might say that the baby isn't really frightened but only anxious, because there is certainly no danger. But the baby cannot determine whether or not this strange new stimulus, a face with glasses, is dangerous. The baby will eventually learn not to be afraid of grandma or her glasses.

"Strangeness" continues to be a cause of anxiety and fear throughout our lifetime. It occurs in racial, religious, ethnic, and social prejudices when we fear the "strangeness" of others because they don't look or act like we do. When we react in this manner, we behave somewhat like the baby who fears the grandmother because of her glasses. We too have to learn that the superficial appearances and insignificant externals of others should not frighten us.

There are other reasons for small children to feel anxious. They live as Lilliputians in a land of giants. They are physically as well as emotionally dependent on the will and, one might add, on the whims of the adults in their lives. We are all sensitive to situations in which we feel someone else is in control of us and of our lives. Even though we look for security in this age of terrorism, we are cautious about government intrusion into our personal information and government surveillance of our private communications. Any arrangement that suggests control by others causes us to feel anxious. Do you doubt that children feel the same in their dependent circumstances? It is difficult to be sure what they feel at times, but we do know that children as young as age 3 or 4 often say to adults "Let me do it. I want to do it." They want to get their own plate from the cabinet before they can reach it. They want to button their own jacket before they are able to do it. They want to walk across the street without the parent's hand before it is safe to do so. Their marked determination to be independent suggests that being dependent causes some unpleasant feelings.

Although small children regularly indicate their desire to "do it myself," for years they remain physically dependent on others. Many doorknobs are beyond their reach. Many windows only show them the sky because they must look up to look out. In early years most chairs are too high to sit on without help. Objects tip over in their presence because the child is poorly coordinated. Eating is tedious because spoons have a way of turning upside down. Most of us have at some time seen a physically handicapped person trying to open a door, move to another chair, pick up a fragile object, or eat a meal in a restaurant. We can be very sensitive to an adult who is so physically limited, but we rarely think about the physical limitations of children. Handicapped adults obviously have a much greater and different burden than the physically limited child, so I would not begin to make any comparison between the two from their perspectives. Many of us have seen the frustration of a person with a speech impediment trying to make someone understand what they are saying. If you have traveled in a foreign country, you may have had the experience of trying to be understood when you didn't have many words in that language to explain yourself. It is frustrating. Perhaps a child finds it frustrating to explain something to an adult who presumes the child has a command of the language the adult speaks.

Children have to learn to distinguish and interpret sounds as well as words. All loud sounds are likely to startle children, whether the sound comes from a slammed door, a broken window, a blaring car radio, or a clap of thunder. With time they learn what various sounds are and whether or not they mean danger. Words can also create anxiety for children who may not understand their meaning or may not be able to interpret the intent of the speaker. I remember when I was 4 or 5 years old coming home from a community picnic with my parents and my siblings in the old model T Ford. As we went through a small town, a train was stopped at the depot, and we had to wait to cross the tracks. There were no other cars waiting. My father said something to my mother, indicating that he was considering driving into the train so it would move. I was frightened but said nothing. I had no realization that my father was joking or that the idea was preposterous. My father was, of course, unaware of my fear. I would not suggest that parents need to filter their speech carefully when children are present. I only wish to make the point again that having an awareness of how children think and feel has considerable benefit for parents.

Even words that are understood by children can be misleading and create apprehension. Commonplace expressions can be confusing. When a person dies, people often say that the person "went to sleep." They may use the words in speaking to young children. "Grandma has gone to sleep and will not be back." They also refer to the family cat or dog being "put to sleep." The child knows that, just like grandma, the cat or dog is not coming back. Is it surprising if the child becomes frightened and starts screaming when being told that, "It's time to go to sleep"? This may occur soon after grandma's passing, or the child may be cooperative at bedtime for weeks and then suddenly make a connection between going to sleep and "never coming back." Of course, the child is unable to explain to the parents why bedtime has become such an anxiety provoking event.

In the late 80's I was involved in arranging an annual symposium on mental health issues at Taylor Manor Hospital in Ellicott City, Maryland. We were fortunate to be able to get the prominent author, Harriet Goldhor Lerner, Ph.D., to be a guest speaker on several occasions. Doctor Lerner has achieved world recognition for her many books, some of which are recognized as "The Dance" books because of their titles. After our first meeting we maintained contact for many years, and I am a great admirer of her work. I was honored when she sent me (for my new granddaughter) a copy of the book she authored in collaboration with Susan Goldhor, "What's So Terrible about Swallowing an Apple Seed?" (Harper Trophy Books, N.Y. 2001) It is a delightful book for children. It also has value for parents because it provides a helpful insight into the mind of a child. On the back cover, Doctor Lerner notes the true story about swallowing an apple seed when she was quite young. Her older sister told her that an apple tree would grow inside her stomach. Although the tree did not grow, her anxieties did, and she imagined all the complications involved as the tree grew bigger and bigger. At some point, her sister repented and gave her the consoling news that she was not, in fact, "expecting a tree." It is difficult for adults even to imagine some of the wild and random ideas and fears that children can create for themselves.

The child's world is full of change and uncertainty. When adults retire for the night they typically have plans for the next day and know what to expect when they awaken in the morning. Pre-school children rarely know what the next day will bring. They are more likely to go to sleep thinking about what they did that day rather than what they will be doing the next. Life is extremely unpredictable when a child is age 2 or 3 or even age 5 or 6. Researchers tell us that change is stressful whether it is positive or negative, and they measure the level of emotional well-being on the scale of life changes. Even if young children are taken to a baby sitter five days a week, they confront changes there in peer group, staff, or activities that are unexpected.

Various family events or changes in parental schedules typically cause at least temporary adjustments in the child's routines. There are illnesses and deaths in extended family, friends, or neighbors. There are job changes and moves to another area. There are major purchases and home repairs and alterations. All of these events can have an impact on the child. Parents may be reluctant to talk to their children about things that are happening in the family or in the neighborhood. If something is happening that the children will hear about and wonder about, they will be less anxious if their parents tell them about it in advance and in a calm and reassuring manner.

I talked with a woman recently who told me that in her childhood she never had any advance notice, explanation, or understanding of plans her family made. She lived in Philadelphia with her mother and maternal grandparents. One of the adults would suddenly (or so it seemed) decide they should all go to Washington to visit relatives. They would leave within 10 to 20 minutes of the announcement. There was no pattern to the visits, and there never seemed to be any particular reason to go or not to go. She never heard any discussion among the adults about anything. To her, life seemed to have no planning. It was all spontaneous, abrupt, and disruptive. It was not unusual to be taken out of a Saturday afternoon movie because the family had decided to go to Washington. The family changed residences on four separate occasions during her early years. Each move was as much of a surprise as the trips were. The unpredictability of life made her uneasy. She felt helpless and insignificant, swept along by the current of adult decisions. Even now she becomes anxious when her spouse or a friend announces a sudden change in plans. She wants to know in advance and be able to plan for things she is going to do.

How do children react when they are anxious? They may talk louder and more. They may fidget and be restless. They may be more opposed to going to bed. They may sleep poorly and have nightmares. When we close our eyes at night, the world becomes less stable, and our worries and fantasies become more real. Adults and children often deal with anxiety by becoming ritualistic. This is quite common in children. When we are anxious our world seems to be "coming apart." If everything seems to be unpredictable and uncertain, we search for a way to establish organization and control. We bring about order by arranging our desk, the kitchen, or the medicine cabinet in a precise manner. It is a token behavior to prove to ourselves that we do have control, that we are still in charge, and that everything is not coming apart.

Several years ago, my wife and I were babysitting our 18 month old granddaughter for the first time. She permitted her parents to leave without a great deal of fuss. As soon as they were gone she went over to the hearth where one of her toys was sitting. It consisted of five or six wooden train cars and a short section of train track. She put all the cars in order on the track one by one, and then she proceeded to take them off in the same methodical manner. She repeated this ritualistic maneuver six or seven times, slowly, precisely, deliberately. After the five minutes or more that the exercise took, she moved about the room and interacted playfully with us and was fine for the rest of the evening. She went to bed and to sleep easily. We thought it was a successful evening. I wonder how well it would have gone had we tried, as soon as her parents went out, to interact with her persistently and intrusively. As I write this, I discovered another possible truth. Perhaps she sensed a certain tension on our part since it was our first "sit" with her. Maybe she was intuitively giving us some time to calm ourselves! She was, of course, a very bright child.

Anxious children are likely to want to straighten out some small part of their world before going to sleep. Shoes go in a very precise arrangement with socks participating in the precision drill. The chair needs to be in a certain spot facing a certain way. The closet door must be open but only a fixed amount. The doll or the teddy bear must be on the shelf in front of the bracket at the left end and looking toward the bed. There is a sense of control and reassurance for the child who can be sure that shoes and socks, chair and door, doll or teddy bear will be there in the morning exactly where they were left the night before. Parents often think such behavior is a ruse to delay bedtime, and it could be so at times, but it may also be a response to the anxieties that darkness spreads through the house and that separation from parents brings.

It might be an appropriate time to give some thought to what often happens to all of us when we awaken at night with some worry on our mind. We have all had nights when we could not get to sleep for a long time or when we woke intermittently. Isn't it remarkable how things can look so bad in the dark, not visually but emotionally bad? If some minor thing disturbed us during the day, it becomes greatly magnified when we reexamine it in the dark. It seems as if we truly cannot see it clearly at that time. When morning comes we often decide it wasn't worth being concerned about, or we relegate it to a less dramatic level. The "bad dreams" that awaken children (and often their parents) are evidence that they too can take happenings of the day to bed with them.

For most children some nighttime rituals persist into their adolescent years and sometimes beyond. If you give it much thought, you will probably become aware that you have some bedtime rituals that are not simply hygienic or utilitarian. Brushing your teeth, locking the door, checking the thermostat are all appropriate activities. But do you need to have your clothes hung with the hangers facing a certain way and the same distance between them? Must your shoes be in a particular place before you can go to sleep? Does the table lamp have to be sitting at the same angle every night? Do you check the locked door only once or are three times necessary?

An interesting secondary effect of ritualistic behavior is that it tends to continue even when the external stimuli and the internal anxiety are no longer present. The bedtime rocking rituals of small children sometimes persist into adolescence. The orderly rituals of adults are sometimes the residuals of childhood behavior. It is interesting in therapy with adults to discover behaviors that are clearly repetitious of earlier patterns. One of the most striking findings with an adult is to learn that this person's current life situation repeats the same emotional climate which was experienced as a child. This search for the familiar is referred to as repetition compulsion.

Life often becomes a balance between holding onto the familiar and exploring the new. Children repeatedly confront this dichotomy. When very young they cling to mother but begin slowly to reach out to connect with others. They may have their favorite stuffed animal from which they can't be separated. Then some other attraction comes along, and they leave the stuffed animal on their bed while they explore a new toy. Curiosity, which will become a driving force in their lives, motivates them as it motivates all of us to expand present interests, to explore other things, to investigate further what is already known.

Overprotective parents can frustrate these natural desires by holding the child back from their desire to move beyond constraining boundaries. One of the ways in which parents can bring this about is by too many warnings. "You might fall, if you do that." "You'll get hurt, if you try that." "Something bad might happen, if you go there." "Be careful." "You may get lost." Undoubtedly there is need for parents to warn children about certain dangers and that should be done calmly and with as much explanation as is appropriate for the situation. But parents who are consistently anxious about their children getting injured or lost or stolen are likely to communicate the anxiety more strongly than they communicate the warning. As a result, they may have an anxious child who isn't sure what to be anxious about, so she or he becomes anxious about everything. Then the child lets fear dispel curiosity, and a major influence on healthy psychological development is lost.

We have learned that children feel insecure because the world is so large and so overwhelming, and they are so small and so weak; because they don't understand a lot of things that they see and hear and touch; and because the emotions of those around them spill over into them. Security comes initially from the mother and her responses to the child's needs. Frequent physical contact between the two is important especially during the first year of life. The mother's sensitivity to the baby's signals creates and sustains a feeling of trust. As the child matures the supportive responses of parents and later other adults continue to be a positive experience. Consistency in parental support provides a background for the child's expanding horizons. At the same time a regulated environment provides the occasion to learn the expectations of maturation and the boundaries of the enlarging world.

Most parents are surprised when the child suddenly crosses the threshold between being a cuddly, pliable infant and becoming a person with definite likes and dislikes and a will which now is often a "won't." Boundaries that are firm, consistent, and fair give the growing child a sense of stability and security. Boundaries are established by parental decision. However, parental decision is appropriately based on sensitivity to the child's current development and attitude as well as to the demands of the situation and its significance for the future. The Swiss psychologist, Piaget, described what he called egocentrism in children under the age of 7. He based this on research showing that children of this age period found it very difficult to accept the point of view of another person over their own. One must conclude that the child's point of view should be heard, but the parent's point of view should prevail.

One of the students I recently taught reported on a case in which she was involved. The student was an intern at a rehabilitation center for drug addicts. Many of the clients were unwilling to acknowledge their need for the program, and even if they did admit that it might be helpful, they were quick to point out how well they were doing and then push to be discharged. Some were there under court order and thus unable to leave until they obtained staff approval for their departure. My student had a client who was pressing to go and needed staff approval in order to obtain release. The student was of the opinion that the client was not ready for discharge, and when asked by the social worker for her recommendation, she gave her honest but negative opinion. Later when she told the client what she had done, the individual was grateful to her for giving that opinion because she felt that it meant the intern cared about her. The student was surprised at the client's positive response to what she had done. I think this is a simple but very telling story because it is such a clear example of how important it is for those in charge to do what is right. Children learn early these days to say "I hate you" to the parent who does not acquiesce to some unseemly demand of the child. I don't recall ever seeing a youngster in therapy who failed to recognize the love involved in sound parental guidance and loving correction.

The intent in this chapter has been to keep the discussion primarily on the emotional life of children. We could not leave the scene without bringing up again one of the paramount "driving forces of human nature" as it pertains to children. That is curiosity.

The curiosity of children is fascinating to watch and inspiring to consider. It is like watching a flower unfold and reveal its inner beauty. It seems to go beyond where we have ever been and to uncover pieces of the world we have long ago forgotten. It is so calm and at the same time so exciting that it takes our breath away. If you do not remember this other world, take a walk with a 2 year old or a 4 year old and listen. You usually don't need to respond. "Where do the birds come from?" "Why does the tree bend that way?" "Where did the stars go?" "Why did that leaf fall?" A tiny rock, the size of a pea, is a treasure to take home. A little stick, now "a tree", is another treasure. A crack in the sidewalk becomes an exploration site. And the world of people and food and things to be done fades off into the shadows, and for a short time you live in a land that is too real to be your imagination and too beautiful to ever leave. You haven't fully known life until you have taken a walk with a child. Do it often!

It is their curiosity that rockets them forward in a learning curve that is beyond what they will ever experience again. They quickly go from questions that often seem more like a mystical comment on life to questions that force adults to put into simple words things they seem never to have thought of in simple terms. "Where did I come from?" "What makes my hair grow?" "Where does the food go when I eat?" "Why did you shout at daddy?" "How long have you been alive?" The answer to the latter may be, "Since we took a walk the other day."

The curiosity of children is nurtured in numerous ways these days. One might wonder if their curiosity has become a focal point for corporate interests. On April 2, 2006 an article by Margaret Webb Pressler appeared in the Business Section of the Washington Post. The article referred to quickly fading interest young children exhibit for their toys, and as a result, they want to move on to more sophisticated toys. The manufacturers are scrambling to create toys to keep the market humming and to keep pace with the creeping boredom that children experience with over-exposure. One might question whether children have the time to appreciate one toy before they are enticed onward to the next. Is it possible that this pattern of attraction to each new product causes an early rejection of the barely used toy and dulls the sense of discovery and excitement which accompanies healthy curiosity? By the time one reaches adolescence, curiosity may be so dulled that "life sucks" because of boredom. Has continued learning lost its luster for many satiated adolescents?

As parents well know, children experience anger. Parents are reluctant to acknowledge that they are often the primary target for the child's anger. A mother may note that her infant's cry signaling hunger or discomfort has turned to a cry of anger when the mother's response has been too long delayed. Time passes quickly, and soon the cry of anger is coming from a toddler when needs are not met or when parental decisions are enforced. Before long the parent becomes a verbal target in the clash of wills. This is often the point at which parents lose their patience and retaliate with anger of their own. There is the temptation to take the position that the child's anger is unjustified, and parental anger is legitimate. In reality, anger does not need to be justified any more than feelings of hunger or pain need to be. It is futile for parents to try to enforce the idea that children should not get angry at parents. In fact, such a position may be dangerous because it does not stop the anger but only drives it underground. What is really important is how anger is expressed. If it cannot be expressed by crying, saying some harsh words, slamming a door, or throwing a pillow; it will be expressed by hitting a younger child, breaking something when no one is around, damaging the neighbor's property, or behaving badly in school.

If anger smolders within the child, it can lead to childhood depression and possible self-harm. Anger is relational. It is directed toward someone. If the person toward whom it is directed is "off limits" to anger, then it is likely to be directed toward someone else or toward oneself. It does not just go away. Anger carries with it the feeling of wanting to hurt the object of the anger. If the anger is transferred to a smaller child or oneself, inflicting hurt can follow. Anger in children is the natural expression of an innate emotional response. Everyone needs to learn how to release anger without doing harm to oneself or others. Childhood is an appropriate time to begin to learn how that is done.

Young children experience sadness for the same basic reasons that adults do. Absence of family members, disappointments, or unpleasant responses from friends can cause gloomy feelings. Parents want to see their child happy. As a result, they may try to compensate in some way for the child's sadness. The reality is that life is not always wonderful, and people are not always happy. Parents can recognize and accept the child's feelings, or they can try to talk them out of it and hold up a rather false picture of life.

When a young child reports that another child was hurtful on the playground, the parent may try to smooth it over, interpret it differently to the child, minimize it, or question the child's role. "She didn't really mean it." "Why didn't you tell the teacher?" "What did you do to her?" "How did it start?" When someone has hurt you, don't you just want to have someone listen to what happened? You want to tell your side of the story, and for now that's the only side that concerns you. You want understanding, sympathy, and support. Later on you can think about or talk about the rest of it. A child has many different feelings. They belong to the child and the child has to learn to deal with them. Parents can encourage the child to accept the feelings they have as part of life and part of their engagement in living. Parents can help children learn to deal with feelings by acknowledging their own emotions and by permitting children to experience and to express theirs.

CHAPTER III

The Adversity of Adolescence

The dictionary defines adversity as "difficulties, misfortune." Adolescence is certainly not a misfortune, but it does involve difficulties. We addressed the previous chapter to the challenge of children, meaning the challenge confronting children. We address this chapter not to the difficulties that parents of teenagers face but to the teenagers themselves and the problems they face in this period of their life. The goal of the chapter is not so bold as to expect young people to read it. The hope is that parents who read it will, as a result, be better able to read their children and have an increased appreciation of youthful responses to the opening vistas of freedom, independence, and responsibility. In addition, this chapter is built on the faith that when youth are treated with respect, understanding, and kindness, they will establish themselves as responsible and caring young adults.

The theme of this chapter is taken from the story of David and Lisa. The novel was written by a psychiatrist, Theodore Isaac Rubin, and in 1962 was made into a film directed by Frank Perry. The story involves two adolescents in a psychiatric institution. Lisa will only speak in rhymes and is reluctant to engage in conversation at all. David reaches out to her with rhymes and entices her to enter into a fragile relationship. A very touching scene between them is repeated several times. Lisa timidly asks, "What do you see when you look at me?" David's response is always the same, "A pearl of a girl."

I believe that every teenager is asking the world Lisa's question, "What do you see when you look at me?" David's response is an ideal one. He makes no claim on her, for he might have said, "Someone I care about, someone I love." He indicates her value but not as value for him. Her value is in herself, and it is hers. She stands alone as "a pearl of a girl." He maintains her integrity as a separate, distinct person. He might have provided a number of qualifiers, "I see someone who is beautiful" or "bright" or "clever" or "interesting." How often do any of us, parent or not, see a teenager as "a pearl of a person?" It is more likely that we see a teen as a good son, a beautiful daughter, a bright student, a good athlete, or a hard worker. It isn't easy to see adolescents separate from our expectations of what we want them to be and our preconceptions about what young people should be. We see teens as part of "our world" which, of course, they are. But we want to fit them into our world according to our desires, our needs, our dreams, and our time table. It is difficult for adults to understand that young people can be very uncomfortable in "the world according to adults."

In preparation for this chapter I researched a number of statistics regarding adolescents. However, I decided not to quote statistics because they do nothing to help us understand any particular adolescent who is asking, "What do you see when you look at me?" Statistics can provide a dark and somber backdrop to use in evaluating an individual. The number of accidental deaths of teenagers tells us of their impulsiveness and their daring. The incidence of venereal diseases and unplanned pregnancies tells us of their passion and need for companionship. Data regarding drug and alcohol abuse tell us of their loneliness and fear. The media stories of adolescent crime tell us of their anger and their pain. The youth who make up this segment of the statistical backdrop have the same emotions, the same sensory abilities, and the same intellectual powers that successful adolescents have.

We search for reasons why the youth of the negative statistics are different than the young people we know. "They were poor." "They experienced abuse as children." "Their parents were separated." "Their father was in prison." "Their face was disfigured." "They had a poor education." When a teenager has committed a terrible crime, the news media always want to find the reason for this aberration. No one dares to think that just being an adolescent involves such frightening possibilities. One statistic is worth stating. Studies have indicated that over 95% of successful adults, as adolescents, engaged in behaviors similar to those for which adolescents currently are arrested.

The period of adolescence is a perilous time because there is a thin line that divides healthy maturation from behavior that can be highly destructive to self and others. A tragic teenage act may indeed be influenced by years of poverty, lack of educational opportunity, abuse, or family disruption; but we must not lose sight of the reality that the emotions of youth are powerful, the behavior of youth is often impulsive, and the judgment of youth is easily impaired. Sometimes this constellation of youthful realities is all we have to explain the behavior that defies our adult frame of reference. I have for a long time believed that one of the problems adults have in trying to understand young people is the fact that adults generally do not remember the frightening, secretive, lonely times of their own youth. And if they were to remember, those memories might disturb their dreams and haunt their waking hours. Therapy with adults often takes them back to rediscover their adolescent years when their interpretation of life, their view of themselves, and their connection with certain others went awry.

The child is ushered into adolescence by two physiologic events. The first of these is a marked growth spurt, and the second is an alteration in hormones. The female begins the production of ova with accompanying menstrual cycles. The male begins to produce sperm. These changes are of considerable physical significance. However, the development of secondary sex characteristics is a more obvious and far more significant psychological event. The period of rapid growth and the onset of these sexual changes are hormonally orchestrated. They represent clear and inescapable evidence to the youth that something very significant has begun to happen.

No matter how much they have been told, no matter how much they have been prepared, this period of transition from childhood to adulthood is one of the most crucial and most mysterious experiences a person will ever have. It is so awesome and so significant that it almost parallels birth. The teen is pushed out of the nest of childhood as a result of physiological and psychological processes occurring at puberty. However, the youngster must also act as midwife for the transition because others cannot initiate or direct the procedure but can only stand aside and help in limited ways.

The period of rapid growth creates problems and anxieties for the adolescent. Some of these are reminiscent of early childhood issues. Size becomes a factor to which the adolescent must adjust. Rapid growth can cause clumsiness which in turn can be embarrassing. A budding teen reaches for something and knocks it over because his or her arm is longer than it was a few weeks ago. Clothing is suddenly too short or too tight, and the wearer feels ill at ease, out of place, and awkward. The situation is similar to that of small children who grow so fast that clothing fits them only for a short time. But teenagers are extremely self-conscious about how they look and what they wear. The world that seemed to fit them in their childhood has quickly changed because they have changed, and it is no longer comfortable.

In addition to the problems caused by growth of trunk and limbs, there is also the development of secondary sex characteristics. Sexual changes are produced by the gonadotropic hormones of the anterior pituitary gland. These hormones simulate the ovaries of the girl to produce ova and the testes of the boy to produce sperm. Masculinizing and feminizing hormones are produced. In the male the penis enlarges, pubic and axillary hair growth occurs, shoulders broaden, and a beard begins to grow. Boys boast about a few whiskers and are proud to display the change in muscle mass. Adults have no problem commenting on these changes and remarking about them to the male adolescent.

Girls are not so fortunate in our society, and because of adult attitudes many girls in early adolescence try to minimize their developing breasts, their rounding hips, the increasing measurement of the pelvic region, and the growth of pubic and axillary hair. This may be a major contributor to the eating disorders of young females. If girls are comfortable enough to change their attire in a manner that shows these feminizing changes, adults are not likely to comment. So girls go through this time of heightened sensitivity to their appearance wondering, "What do you see?" How can young women feel comfortable about their bodies when adults are too uncomfortable to talk about the changes that are occurring? There is no difficulty talking about a boy's display of masculinity because we do not associate it directly with sexual behavior. It seems otherwise for girls.

One of the healthy ways in which adolescents cope with these dramatic changes is to talk to one another. They become uncomfortable talking to adults, partly because they sense that adults become uncomfortable with them. Youth need to converse with someone, and the most approachable someone is another teenager. There is a great deal of value in these conversations among teens. First of all, by talking they objectify their concerns. When we put an apprehension or anxiety into words it is less likely to grow. When we give it voice it exists outside us, and we can view it in a more detached manner. It is in conversations with other teens that the youth discovers that she or he is not "crazy" because of certain thoughts, not "vile" because of certain feelings, and not "wicked" because of certain behaviors. It is not unusual to hear adult patients "confessing" some teenage thoughts or behaviors which have burdened them for years because they believed them to be so weird, so sordid, or so evil. One concludes that these adults never had the corrective experience of adolescent talk sessions.

The physical changes already mentioned become a major source of anxiety for teenagers and focus their attention on their bodies. Parents are often annoyed by the resulting preoccupation with their appearance. Teens spend hours in the bathroom. Preparation for leaving the house can become a ritual of dressing and preening with the end result being less than desirable from the parents' point of view. Parents usually monitor and direct the styles and standards of their younger children. But teenagers develop styles and standards of their own. Fashion designers are quick to respond to any evidence of changing patterns in adolescent dress, and before parents can catch their breath, there is new merchandise in the stores and in the magazines with the latest in teen fads. There are other teens who deal with their "body-image anxiety" by trying to ignore the physical changes that are occurring. They continue to dress as preadolescents and pay no attention to the fads, sometimes wearing unseemly outfits. But when they dress to rebel against what teens find fashionable, it seems that another fad is often created.

Although pubertal girls may initially hide their developing feminine contours, when they do accept the changes they tend to dress in fashions that clearly demonstrate their more mature figure. Present day styles for teen girls are considerably more revealing than they were some years past. Current fashions may cause critical glances and negative comments from adult observers who are more concerned with "how much do I see" than with "what do I see." As a result of these adult reactions, the young person may become more extreme in dress. Another result of teen fashions seems to be that younger women and younger mothers find these styles attractive and take them for themselves. When this happens, adolescent girls are prone to move on to something different and perhaps more daring. Teenagers are not about to adopt what is in vogue for adults, and if adults adopt the teen fashions, the adolescent will choose something else.

Adolescents want to separate themselves from adults, and in our culture they have certainly taken their position as a distinct group. They have become a focus group for a large share of the advertising dollar. They have their music, their dance, their idols, their vocabulary, and their styles of dress and behavior. They are the celebrity makers for some stars and some musicians. When we watch a show on television which features one of their idols, we usually see several mothers and occasionally fathers waving and jumping and screaming along with the teenagers. I often wonder if the parents are there because they like the music, because they are trying to recapture something from the past, or because they think it is important to share this experience with their child.

Parents usually engage in all kinds of activities with their preadolescent children, believing that this creates closer bonds and is supportive of the child's healthy psychological development. And they are correct. The same is not true of adolescent development. Adolescents are in the process of separating from parents, of finding their own path, of establishing their own identity. Some parents remain too intrusive in the lives of their teens and are reluctant to permit teenagers to distance themselves gracefully and productively.

The term "teenager" covers a wide range of age and of development. It is ridiculous to have the same standards for a 13 year old and a 17 year old. A few years ago I treated Jeff, a 17 year old college student, who was being held to 13 year old standards by his father. The father insisted that he know where his son went and with whom he spent time after school. On occasion the father would call the house of one of Jeff's friends to see if he was there. This young man had never openly opposed his father's behavior and consequently was having some serious difficulty in establishing his own identity. I encouraged the father to see a colleague of mine who could help him understand the need his son had to make decisions appropriate for a 17 year old.

My patient's ability to express his independence developed rapidly with brief therapy. In our work it became clear that his father had some concerns regarding his son's sexual orientation, evident from his father's probing questions and continued intrusive attitude. Jeff was aware of the parental concern, and he found it disconcerting because he felt uncertain about his own sexual preferences. The major influence which the father had exerted on Jeff through his formative years was apparent. The son had looked to his father as his guide, and he had maintained the attitude that "father knows best." Now he felt that he faced a dilemma. His father seemed to believe that he was gay, and he was wondering if the idea had been planted in his head by his father's attention to it or if indeed he was gay.

With the benefit of his therapy, the father began to retreat from his meddling as he acknowledged that his attachment to his son met a growing need he had in his life. Jeff was their only child. His mother had a position that demanded long hours of work. The father worked an early morning shift and was home by 2 PM. He liked his son's companionship, and he was feeling rather resentful because Jeff was spending increasing amounts of time with his friends. Jeff began to take a more decisive attitude about his time, his friends, and his behavior. He was still pondering the question of his sexual orientation as he left therapy.

Parents who maintain rigid boundaries and interfering attitudes toward developing teenagers will either warp their emotional growth or stimulate dangerous revolt. Most people are well aware of the extremes of adolescent rebellion. They read about it in the newspapers, and they hear about it on television. They witness it in the malls and in the street, and they hear about it from friends. They refer to them as "street kids", gang members, "punks," delinquents, or criminals. Some youth may be all of those, but they may also be "just teens" with different hair cuts, multiple body piercings, loud boom boxes, or outlandish make-up. These latter behaviors are annoying to adults, but for the most part, they represent young people confronting the expectations of their elders in a harmless gesture of defiance. Adolescents would be offended to have this called rebellion because from their point of view it is a matter of style and good taste.

Youth who rebel against narrow limits and invasive monitoring are more likely to become healthy adults than are those who remain docile and obedient throughout their developing years. It is sad to see a young adult living the life of an overgrown and outdated teenager. In recent years my practice has indicated that there are an increasing number of young adults, more typically males, who have not left the nest. They continue to live at home sometimes attending a few college classes, sometimes having a part time job, and sometimes doing neither. They tend to become reclusive and often spend a great deal of their time playing video games. It is possible that in their adolescent years they were influenced by the cautious parameters or self-serving expectations of parents. They no longer fit in the world outside the home because they no longer exhibit age appropriate interests or behaviors. They are young adults who failed the essential psychological development of their adolescence.

Not long ago, at the request of a worried mother I saw her 26 year old son for a psychiatric evaluation. She was concerned that he seemed unable to find a regular job. He was an only child and had always lived at home with his mother. His father died when he was six years old. On interview he was pleasant, cooperative, and quite frank in telling me about himself. He had average grades through his high school years. He did not play sports and had not participated in any school activities. He had several friends during high school years but had not maintained contact with them. He denied any abuse of alcohol or drugs. During her telephone call to set up the appointment his mother told me that he had been attending a few college classes every year since he finished high school. When I asked him how his classes were going, he acknowledged readily that he was not attending college and never had attended. He told his mother that he was taking classes so that she would give him money for tuition and books, money which he spent for personal needs. He had obtained three or four different part time jobs over the years, but none of these held any interest for him nor did they last very long.

Although he did not exhibit any clear psychiatric symptoms, I thought there might be some benefit in a few visits to explore further his lack of motivation and his deceitful exploitation of his mother. He declined the invitation. I suggested that it might be appropriate for him to return with his mother to see me at least one more time. Naturally and expectedly he again declined. He was aware that I could not reveal any of this to his mother without his permission. In retrospect, I'm not certain his mother would have wanted to know the truth, or perhaps she already did know it at some level but did not want to admit it to herself.

In spite of what they portray to others, young people typically have very little confidence in themselves. In the prior chapter we noted how three year olds will confidently say to helping adults, "Let me do it," often before they are ready to do it. After they try and fail, they will let the adult take over. Adolescents have a difficult time indicating that they want help or accepting help from adults because they often doubt their own abilities. It is easy for them to ask adults for all kinds of services or for things they need. "Will you fix my breakfast?" "Bring me a pen." "Take me to my friend's house." "Will you find my coat?" "Will you fix my bike?" These are all things that they either know they can do or things that they are not interested in trying to do.

It is a different story when they face something that is entirely new, something which stirs their hidden doubts about themselves. Did you ever try to teach a teenager how to drive? Many of them have difficulty adjusting to a learning mode when it comes to cars. They have dreamed of the day when they can drive, and in preparation they have carefully watched their parents and perhaps their friends drive. They know how it's done, and they have imagined themselves doing it dozens of times. They have convinced themselves that it is easy to do, and when it is more complex than envisioned they teeter on the edge of failure. For an adolescent with all the secret self-doubts that is a very uncomfortable place to be especially with a parent watching. It is not quite so bad if it is only a driving instructor who is present. If they fail, they doubt themselves even more, and it becomes more difficult for them to accept help from an adult.

The parents of a 17 year old in his last year of high school made an appointment for him to see me. He was a quiet young man with a pleasant smile which rarely appeared. He was doing well in school but had few friends and said he preferred to keep to himself. He was planning to go away to college. He had a girl friend whom he had been seeing for about six months and who planned on going to the same college. He expressed little enthusiasm for any of these plans. Actually he showed little zest for anything in his life. He was sleeping poorly and having some frightening dreams which he would not further describe. One of his future plans was to move to one of the Balkan countries after graduating from high school. He had little reason for the choice other than to say that most of the people there used bicycles to get around, and he had never learned to drive a car. He said that he had taken the driver's test twice when he was 16 and had failed on both occasions. He refused even to consider taking the test again. He had convinced himself that he really had no desire and no need to drive.

However, the driving failure was undoubtedly the precipitating cause of his current depression. His self-esteem seemed irrevocably damaged. Suicide was frequently on his mind especially when he faced his failure in the dark of night. About this same time he began sleeping with a light on in his room. Antidepressant medication with continuing therapy was helpful. He slept better, acquired a more optimistic attitude about the future, and began to interact with a wider range of peers at school. He discontinued therapy sometime before graduation, although he agreed to continue the antidepressant for an additional three months. We never discussed driving again, but I felt that his broader association with others, his expanding horizons, and his increasing self-confidence would eventually get him behind the wheel.

We quoted Piaget as saying that children have a difficult time accepting the point of view of someone else. A teenager has difficulty accepting the point of view primarily of parents and secondarily of anyone who sounds like their parents. Adolescents want to do things for themselves, and one of those things is to think for themselves. It is not unusual for teens to overshoot the mark because they are more comfortable with black and white than they are with grey. Grey includes both sides of an issue. Teens see things in absolutes because they doubt themselves when faced with ambiguity. Consequently they are attracted to people who take positions different than their parents, especially if those people tend to be radical and dogmatic. This quality makes them vulnerable to the fanatic and the extremist whether in politics, religion, entertainment, or fashion.

Anna Freud maintained that one of the major struggles for this age group was to modify their erotic interest in the parent of the opposite sex. Many consider that an extreme position, but there is marked evidence of a change in behavior between parents and teens, normally initiated by the youngster. Children who were physically affectionate typically decrease their physical contact with parents, especially the parent of the opposite sex, as they move into adolescence. They become aware that they are no longer "daddy's little girl" or "mama's little boy." Parents are often puzzled by this seeming rebuff and may unconsciously withdraw their affection. Teens may become uncomfortable even with affectionate comments from parents, especially if these occur in the presence of their peers. They may resent it if parents continue to use pet names from childhood years. They are embarrassed by solicitous parents. They do not want to be seen in the child role. Adults are able to let other adults know in a straight forward manner that they care about them and think well of them. Parents might try a similar approach with their adolescents.

Parents of adolescents focus on rules, reports, and respect and in the process lose sight of affection, understanding, and guidance. Young people do need guidance, but lectures are generally not acceptable to them. Parents who provide some facts about a subject and make some recommendations based on those facts help the adolescent think things through. It is the phrase, "think things through," that is essential. That is precisely what they want to do, and in final analysis, it is what we want them to do in order to achieve independent and reliable adulthood. Parents who are determined to convince their teenagers that certain behaviors are wrong or unhealthy or sinful may get obligatory but insincere nods of understanding and acceptance. Youth have difficulty accepting the staid opinion of adults regarding matters that are current, vibrant, and popular for teenagers. They need to be encouraged to think things through and not feel brow beaten.

Another factor in parental guidance is timing. I remember taking one of my sons aside when he was age 9 or 10 to provide some information about sex. During our time together I noted that he seemed to want to ask a question. As I finished what undoubtedly sounded like a lecture to him I asked him if he had any questions. (I was probably hoping the question wouldn't be too incisive.) His question was, "Can I watch the ballgame now?" He was quite a baseball fan, and the game had started half an hour earlier. My timing may have been alright for his age but not for his love of baseball. Parents are more likely to delay guidance than to be premature with it. In this informational age, children as young as age 5 and 6 become acquainted with bits and pieces of information relating to what we might have previously considered discussing with teenagers. "Better too early than too late" is a good position to take in providing parental information and opinion about social conduct, sexual behaviors, and substance abuse issues.

A few years after I finished my training in psychiatry I was seeing a 15 year old youngster from the District of Columbia. He was an only child. His mother and father had high level jobs in the federal government. He was a rather hostile youth who assumed a generally defiant and argumentative attitude during our sessions. He frequently talked about his trips with older companions to "The Strip," a red light district in Baltimore. He bragged about passing as an adult and participating in the entertainment offered in the area. I would occasionally ask him if his parents knew about these forays into the night. His reply was always the same. "My parents won't tell **me** what to do." He talked about coming home at two or three in the morning and waking his parents to let him in the house. It always struck me as incongruous that someone who was old enough to stay out until three in the morning was not old enough to have a key to the house.

During one of our meetings I again commented on his parents' attitude about his behavior. His reply surprised me and was a major turning point in therapy. "My parents **won't tell me what to do.**" They had lectured him at times in the past, but they had not provided guidance that he could think about and discuss with them and make his own. After this insightful comment he became willing to look at his own behavior in a more objective and evaluative manner. As he initiated changes that were positive for him his relationship with his parents improved, and they became more accepting of him and he of them. No matter how oppositional they appear, no matter how argumentative they become, no matter how demeaning they are toward authority, adolescents do want someone to be strong, reasonable, and understanding who will provide guidelines and clear boundaries for them.

Conflict between adolescent and parent is bound to occur if the adolescent is developing appropriately. It is important that the conflict not destroy communication and regular contact. Parents who match hostile comments with hostile comments and sarcasm with sarcasm will turn a quarrel into a war. Teenagers can shut parents out of their lives in a variety of ways. The simplest is to spend all their time in their room. Unfortunately many parents are quite content to let their youngsters fade from the family table, avoid spending time with other relatives or company, and absent themselves from all family activities.

In working with teenagers I have been appalled to learn how many of them live in a household where they rarely have any interaction with the others who live there. It always struck me as very sad that this interesting and dynamic young person that is with me in my office feels so alone and so unappreciated in his or her home. Of course, there is usually a television, a telephone, and a computer in the solitary teen's room to provide companionship.

That fact may be some consolation to the parents, but it did not make me feel any less troubled. Parents have the delicate task of keeping the teen in touch with the family even when the youth is looking to find increasing relationships outside the home. The outside relationships are essential to healthy development, but adolescents need to know and **feel** that they are still part of this family. If communication remains intact, parents and teens can discuss which family gatherings and events will include all the family.

The period of adolescence is a volatile time for many reasons. In addition to the rapid changes in their bodies, their emotions are becoming more powerful and less predictable. The hormonal changes of this period increase the heightened emotional reactivity. Angry outbursts can come with little provocation and can produce a flood of tears, harsh words, screaming, physical violence, running away, or other defiant behaviors. Angry adolescents like angry adults are typically unreasonable as long as they remain angry. Later they may feel embarrassed by their angry outbursts, but if the parent decides to demand an apology, it may rekindle the battle because it clashes with the adolescent's need to save face. We all know how difficult it is to admit we were wrong, to back down from a position we took, to apologize. Apologies are more likely to come spontaneously at a later time when mood is improved and mind is calmer. Parents might also consider whether or not apologies are appropriate from their side of the field.

There are extreme indications of and results from adolescent anger. The news media regularly report on some of these: unprovoked violence toward strangers, graffiti in public places, destruction of property, theft in stores, and other acts of revenge toward the adult world represented primarily by parents and teachers. Anger may also be involved in body piercing, music choices, and extreme styles of hair or of dress. These items do not always portray anger. They may simply represent the adolescent's current presumed good taste, or they may occur because of the youth's need to go along with a group of peers. The choice of peers is often connected with anger toward parents. Why else would the teen so carefully chose exactly those peers to whom the parents are most opposed?

One hears the expression "peer pressure" to indicate how one or more persons exert influence on another person to participate in a certain attitude or behavior, usually considered negative. Peer pressure may exist in the child's world and in the world of adults, but I do not think it is a major factor for adolescents. The reason adolescents join peers in illegal, dangerous, or destructive behaviors is because they feel pressured by their own inner need to belong, to find family replacements, to avoid the dread of loneliness. The anger of adolescents needs to be recognized at its beginning and responded to with caution, with sensitivity, and with sincerity by adults who can listen with patience and respond with love. It must be resolved because if it is not it will become increasingly dangerous and more violent.

In doing therapy with adolescents I have seen anger toward parents manifested in many different ways. Not long after I began my psychiatric practice, I learned something about adolescent anger from a 13 year old patient. Her mother brought her for the first appointment. With a patient this young, my pattern was to see the parent initially, get some basic information, and inquire as to the reason for the appointment. The mother described her daughter as a good girl who got along well with family and peers. She brought Mary to see me because she was failing in school. She had been a very successful student in prior years with straight A's. Except for her grades there were no complaints from the school about her behavior.

I saw Mary and found her to be an attractive, articulate person who was relatively at ease for a first encounter. I obtained some additional information from her and then set up another appointment. She seemed quite willing to return. We continued through several sessions, and she remained friendly and willing to discuss family, friends, and activities. Her father worked for the federal government; her mother was a teacher; and she had an older sister and a younger brother. We talked about her school work from time to time. She presented no definite psychiatric symptoms.

One day in an effort to elicit more understanding of her school problem, I said, "You are a bright girl. You and I know that. The teachers know that and your parents know that. Can you explain to me why you get failing grades when you are bright and could certainly get good grades?" I have never forgotten her reply. "It's quiet anger." She explained that she was angry at her mother because she felt her mother treated her differently than she treated the two siblings. With the girl's permission I had another session with her mother to explore this further. The mother was quite candid. When she was pregnant with this child she discovered that her husband was having an affair. She acknowledged that she had always felt differently toward this daughter. The mother was eager to repair the damage and set out to do so. Her daughter responded well to the mother's change of heart, and school work rapidly improved.

It is not unusual for teenagers to exhibit "quiet anger" toward parents who are too demanding or who seem to be favoring another son or daughter. It is rare to have an adolescent admit the behavior so candidly. There is a second lesson in this case history. It is the story of communication and how subtly it occurs between parent and child (and probably any two people). Neither the daughter nor the mother could give me specific examples of how the mother's attitude was imparted to the girl, but there was no question about it being there, unconsciously to the mother, somehow known to the child. Quiet anger is difficult to recognize and consequently difficult to confront and resolve. It is exhibited in reduced communication, remaining as physically distant as possible, avoiding unnecessary contact, and, most importantly, failing at something that is seen as highly valued by the parent.

More commonly adolescent anger is loud, threatening, frightening, and sometimes violent. I treated an adolescent for several years whose anger toward his parents seemed to be beyond resolution.

I first met him when he was hospitalized for one of several outbursts of anger he had exhibited over a period of several months. In the episode that led to his hospitalization, he had broken furniture in the home, intimidated other family members with his cursing and threatening comments, and physically attacked his father leaving several bruises on the father's face. At the time of the youth's admission, colleagues suggested that he must have a bipolar illness. He had been given that diagnosis in a prior treatment situation. It gradually became evident that he had a severe obsessive compulsive illness. In the present context, I only want to discuss his anger.

After his discharge I continued to see him as an outpatient for several years. Large segments of our therapy sessions were spent on his verbal tirades about his parents. He spoke cruelly and disparagingly of them focusing the worst of his venom on his mother. His expressed wish was that when they are old they will be penniless and have to go to the worst possible nursing home, and he will refuse ever to visit them. On occasion when his parents would be in the waiting room as he came in or left the office, he would continue his contemptuous treatment of them in front of me. As therapy continued he became well enough to begin college and pursue his avid interest in the medical field. He had increasing interaction with peers and began a challenging part time job in a hospital setting. He was appreciated by his coworkers, and he began to experience an independence and self-sufficiency he had never felt before. As he became more involved in other interests, comments about his parents became fewer and less harsh. I will never forget the day his mother called and told me that he had given her a card for Mother's Day with a hand written affectionate note. During his next office visit I mentioned briefly that his mother had called and was pleased that he had given her a card. He made no comment. Although he had retreated from his prior hostility he did not want to acknowledge his change of heart. Teens need to save face even more than adults do.

In the last chapter, we spoke of the driving force of curiosity in children and how it expands their world. With teenagers we find that curiosity is a powerful motivating force and, in this instance, is coupled with the desire for attachment, which will also be referred to as love. The endocrine glands did more than stimulate a growth spurt and produce sexual changes. They also opened up the flood gates on sexual curiosity and sexual behavior. Younger children are curious about sex and frequently engage in rather innocent sexual exploration, but sex does not become a primary force in their behavior until adolescence. To say that adolescents are preoccupied with sex is hardly an exaggeration. Attention to their features, their body shape and size, their clothing, their walk, their voice, their words, and on and on, all is related directly or indirectly to the impression they will make on other teenagers of the opposite or same sex. Their curiosity about sex is intense and far-reaching because sex is an area that seems to hold endless mystery for humans. Even most adults, no matter what exotic or extensive sexual experiences they might have had, still believe they have missed out on some unbelievably wonderful sexual experience that could have been and someday may still be. For some, sadly enough, the search never ends.

Several factors combine to feed the sexual interests of adolescents. Their hormones have been unleashed; they are separating from the bonds of family; they are overwhelmed by the big world they are facing; their bodies are calling attention to their sexual organs; they are seeking connectedness to peers. In addition, there is now a very satisfying pleasure attached to the stimulation of their sexual organs. All of these factors bring adolescents to the satisfactions of exploratory sexual behaviors by themselves or with peers. Masturbation becomes an early outlet for strong sexual feelings. Since sexual satisfaction produces a sense of release and relaxation, it can easily become a kind of refuge from the stresses of life. However, sexual behavior frequently carries with it feelings of guilt and shame associated with restrictions and taboos coming from parents, church figures, and society.

When I was beginning the practice of psychiatry, I remember teenage boys occasionally sharing their fear that masturbating might cause them to become insane. I doubt if that belief is still prevalent, but some youth still have lingering concerns about what masturbation may do to their bodies. It is important that adolescents understand the implications, the complications, the emotional components and the emotional residuals of sexual behaviors. Informative discussions about these matters provide more knowledge than lectures ever will.

Sexual behavior is fundamentally a search for intimacy and is the natural culmination of the closeness and attachment involved in a loving, dedicated relationship. Young people are not psychologically ready for this depth of intimacy because they are still in the process of establishing their own identity. Their self-identification comes from the multiple interactions they have with others in their world and from their ability to evaluate and assimilate what they take from those experiences and make their own. Sexual encounters ideally represent a desire for intimacy, but for teens they are vain attempts to find identity. These liaisons are physically focused, pleasure seeking, self-gratifying events. They tend not to be deeply assuring to the partner, nor do they typically provide a sense of one's inherent value as a person. Although the sexual experience may be physically satisfying, the encounter does not satisfy the identity search; so the adolescent may move on to a series of different partners, seeking that illusive sense of personhood. Promiscuity may result. Similar behavior occurs in some adults and suggests the absence of a secure sense of identity.

There comes a time when feelings that are different than sexual desire begin to surface and focus on a discovered "other." Affection for another and a desire to be with that person begins to take precedence over one's own interests. Then one day, the adolescent has found enough wholeness in self that another can be of greater value than self. The emotion of love is blossoming and will continue to grow for years to come sending out some shoots that will wither and die, branching in many different directions, needing pruning, needing nurturing, needing good ground in which finally to become a tree of life.

A stable sense of self is not easily attained by young people. They are overwhelmed by the freedom of choice which they fight so hard to achieve and defend so strongly. They distrust themselves, their parents, and other authority figures, and they can find betrayal in the ephemeral relationships they develop with peers. They are perturbed by the uncertainty of tomorrow, the fragility of relationships, and the misuse of resources and lives about which adults seem so casual. They face existential fears for which they have no voice. In the last chapter we considered some of the innocent questions of small children looking at a world of marvel and mystery. Looking at a world of decisions and doubts, teens have questions they rarely ask. "Is there a God?" "Why do people fight wars?" "What will life be like when I'm forty?" "What happens after I'm dead?" "Where is my life going?" When I ask teenagers who are "cutters" why they cut themselves, the most common response is that they want "to feel." Is it possible that they think so much they cannot feel, or is it that they feel so much they cannot think? Whatever is happening, they are unable to put it all into words, and they flounder in the tempest of their time. Cutting seems to bring them a sense of identity, a sense of self, a sense of reality. Sometimes they describe it as a way of bringing themselves out of a fog. It is rare that teenagers who cut themselves have serious thoughts of suicide.

Identity issues arise for adolescents who are pressed to decide on careers and what they want to become before they know who they want to be. They sometimes remind me of lemmings as they go rushing off to college because their friends are going or because it is the expectation of parents, grandparents, extended family, or teachers. I have seen a number of them home at midyear or after one year, discouraged, disenchanted, and depressed. Erik Erikson has suggested that some adolescents unwittingly postpone entry into that decision phase of life through "patienthood" or delinquency. I often wonder how much enthusiasm for life, how much natural curiosity, how much hidden talent, and how much creativity have been lost when young people are pushed by others to follow a preconceived path which becomes a dead end street.

It is important for adolescents to have their own goals in life and to pursue the education commensurate with those goals.

This chapter has touched rather briefly on the complexities of adolescent development. The expectation is that these comments will encourage adults who work with teenagers to reflect on the significance of each contact they have with each adolescent they see. There is the hope that the adult will remember the teen's unspoken question, "What do you see when you look at me?" The parent, the teacher, the neighbor, the employer, the policeman, the judge, each one sees the same adolescent differently. Each one imparts a lasting picture, a picture that will become part of that adult in the making.

CHAPTER IV

The Adventure of Adulthood

This chapter title was chosen because it describes this period of life as we should try to think of it. The dictionary defines adventure as "an unusual and exciting, typically hazardous, experience or activity; a daring and exciting activity calling for enterprise and enthusiasm". What could be a better description of adulthood! One's adult life is not only unusual it is unique, the only one of its kind. It is a "one and only life cycle" as several writers describe it. There are exciting times even in the most average life, and hazardous experiences are not uncommon. Everyone faces challenging times which will require perseverance, quiet bravery, heroic effort, and sacrifice. Life expects us to be resourceful and calls us to be enthusiastic.

Adulthood extends over a period of approximately 40 years. Its onset is not as dramatic as was the onset of adolescence. There is no clear demarcation between this stage of life and the preceding one. Specified ages when a person may drive, drink alcohol, consent to intercourse, vote, marry, or serve in the military are attempts in one way or another to indicate a separation between adolescents and adults. These stated ages are not all the same and may vary from state to state.   There are legal definitions of majority, the age when a person is considered an adult under the law. We know that majority does not always coincide with maturity. The transition to adolescence was not defined by a precise age but normally occurs anytime over a two or three year period. The transition to adulthood, if we accept the dictionary definition as "an emotionally and mentally mature individual," can only be assessed on an individual basis. This suggests that maturity requires a certain norm which some persons in this age range do not always meet.

We need to keep in mind that most adults can and do "behave like children" at times. You would probably not have to go too far back in time to recall an incident when you behaved somewhat irrationally, when you were angry and said some things that sounded more like a 5 year old speaking, or when you made some threats that reminded you of something your teenager has said. Perhaps we need to look at maturity more as a standard of behavior we strive for, and when we fail to achieve that goal of "emotionally and mentally mature behavior" we need to right whatever wrongs we have done to others, forgive ourselves for once again missing our goal, and by doing this regain our title of "mature adult."

Making judgments about the maturity of others is a risky thing to do unless we know them quite well and have observed an adequate sample of their behaviors. I recently read an interesting but disturbing book, "Generation Me" (Free Press, N.Y. 2006), by Jean M. Twenge, Ph.D. I kept thinking as I went from page to page, "This is a book about adolescents."   Over the past 50 years I have seen hundreds of adult patients. A minority of them were seriously ill. Most of them were everyday people like you and I meet in class, at work, at church, in stores, or in the neighborhood. They did not strike me as the kind of assertive, entitled, defiant, and undisciplined persons that Twenge describes. Since the book is not about adolescents, I would be inclined to believe that it is about individuals who have not yet matured, hopefully not as large a segment of our population as some of the statistics suggest. If the information in the book is accurate, it indicates that many of these young adults have not reached a developmental level commensurate with our definition of maturity.

We previously indicated that childhood and adolescence were not easy stages to negotiate. Now we can add that the attainment of adult maturity is by no means a simple task. Being fully grown does not instill wisdom. Reaching the age of 18 or 21 does not of itself bring emotional control. Adulthood comes abruptly by legal definition. Maturity comes by lengthy process. We have already noted that the changes occurring in childhood and in adolescence progress over a number of years to reach completion. It takes time to achieve a level of maturity commensurate with the concept of adult. However, complex choices may arise, major decisions may be made, and serious commitments can occur much too early for the evolving adult.

Life takes on a serious and weighty quality for those who enter early into marriage, home buying, and parenthood. Some young people are able to meet the responsibilities of these decisions because they have been making responsible decisions in late teen years and are now setting out to achieve some life goals. Others who enter into marriage and parenthood at an early age are not prepared for the responsibility or the commitment. If they feel overwhelmed by the choices they have made and burdened by the obligations they have assumed, they are likely to make changes with the same immaturity that led them to the earlier decision. They may receive advice from parents, from friends, from counselors, from clergy, and from people they happen to talk to in the grocery store. It can be difficult for them to make a good decision because they are not equipped to do it by themselves, and those who would advise them may either have a vested interest or no real interest--except for the counselor. A good counselor can help them sort through their thoughts, their feelings, and their conflicts and expectations toward one another. Alternatives would be considered and discussed. A decision could be made that would leave each of them with a sense of faith in themselves and in the future rather than a sense of failure. The process might teach them a good deal about maturity and how emotions enter into and sometimes confuse the process of decision making.

There are other decisions with serious consequences that young adults make. One of these is enlistment in the military. Obviously for most young people this is not a lifetime commitment, but it is a choice that can have the awful outcome of death or permanent disability. Youngsters are recruited at age 17 and are approached even before that. Many sign up while still living at home and do so against the expressed wishes of their parents. I am not suggesting that the consent of their parents should be required, but I am suggesting that the act may be a rebellion against the role of family and the rule of parents. The behavior is often similar to the teenager who "runs away to get married," when in reality she or he is running away to get out of the home. In either case the decision may be that of a very immature young person, and the result may be tragic and cause a lifetime of regret.

Another area of early choice with significant consequences is found in the attraction of young people to cults. In the previous chapter we mentioned that adolescents are looking for leaders to replace parental authority and for relationships to supplant family ties. Young adults who have not found these replacements can be attracted to these groups. Their rigid tenets, consuming environment, and brain-washing techniques not only limit independent behavior but curtail individual thought.

Seemingly mature adults can and do make decisions based on faulty judgment and unfettered emotions. Negative consequences can be far reaching. Young adults are more prone to make quick and rash choices. They are more inclined to let emotions lead them, if not drive them, to life-long commitments. Emotional forces such as love, patriotism, or piety may be excessively influential in some decisions. All of these are feelings to be valued, but they must also be evaluated. Reason requires that questions be asked. Is the object of affection a suitable counterpart, or will this relationship be a disastrous union? Is the cause of patriotism a worthy cause in this instance, or is it a blind faith in a misguided or murderous leader? Is the infusion of piety built on strong and reasoned beliefs, or is it a passing desire to change one's life or to change the world? If seasoned individuals owe anything to young people, they owe them the kindness not to push them into decisions they are not ready to make, the generosity not to impose, even subtly, their own expectations on them, the honesty to help them separate emotion from reason, and the grace to acknowledge that they themselves are not perfect and do not have all the answers.

We have considered choices young adults make that are of momentous importance in their lives. The majority of young people opt for less significant goals. They take a path that is not so narrow and not so limiting. Many go to college. Some decide to work for a time before college, and some elect not to consider college in the immediate future. These decisions allow them the freedom to change their minds and take another direction without great loss of time. Unfortunately this interim may extend for several years and on occasion end badly. They may alter their direction several times and grow uncertain of themselves and weary in the pursuit of a career that attracts them. Some of them lose interest in earlier ideas and plans and seem unmotivated to search for alternatives. Perhaps everything came too easily and too quickly before, and now life takes more effort and more determination. Their inability to move forward may be based on consciously or unconsciously trying to pursue the expectations of others and not their own. It may be that parents or teachers have unwittingly burdened them with comments that were meant to encourage but which became an albatross. Words of praise can easily become a measure of success or failure for those who hear them.

I worked with a young man in his mid-20's who carried the burden of a first grade teacher's praise. He was an outstanding young boy, bright, talented, energetic, and enthusiastic. His teacher always spoke of him as, "My Harvard boy." An episode of severe physical illness which led to a lengthy emotional illness left him physically and emotionally weakened, doubting himself, and afraid to confront the demands of everyday life. He was only too keenly aware of the gap between the reality of his situation and the distant world of Harvard. A comment that was undoubtedly meant to inspire and support him had become a stark sign of his failure.

A few years ago a 23 year old male came to see me under the duress of a mother's love. He had been a good student and a star football player in high school. He had just completed two years at a small college in the Northeast. In his senior year of high school his grades dropped precipitously after his football season ended with a torn cartilage in his knee. He began using alcohol at age 12, stealing it from his parents. He had friends buying it for him when he was 14. It became his drug of choice early in life. He began the casual use of marijuana at age 16 and did some experimentation with cocaine and ecstasy in his senior year of high school and at college. The college he attended was well known for its parties. He didn't miss any of them. He was on probation at the end of his first semester, but his intelligence helped him scrape through the spring term and go on to his second year. He continued drinking on a daily basis and on occasion became belligerent toward campus police. The dean asked him not to return at the conclusion of his second year. He returned home and lived with his parents.

In the previous two years he had been working in an office setting where he had conflicts with his supervisor. In therapy he frequently talked about a future football career and about returning to college. When faced with questions about either of these goals, he became defensive and irritated or treated it all with levity. When first in treatment, he was continuing to visit his college about once a month, the visits coinciding with the "big parties." He finally acknowledged the seriousness of his alcoholism, and after several failures of attempted abstinence he agreed to go into a treatment facility. His parents were supportive emotionally and financially. He completed the program and continued in therapy for several months afterwards. When we terminated treatment, he continued in the same mundane job which he correctly considered was beneath his abilities. He dated on occasion but had not established a stable relationship with anyone. He spent a great deal of time watching television or playing video games. College was never mentioned, and football was no longer attractive to him. I had the unpleasant feeling that his dreams had faded, and even though he was only 23 he might never have such dreams again.

The face of psychiatry is changing. During the past few years I have had several parents coming as patients primarily because of their distress and disappointment related to a son or daughter anywhere from age 25 to 35 still living at home almost as a recluse. Apparently these young people had not been able to accomplish the transition from adolescence to adulthood. In the past when a person was called a "drop out" it usually referred to quitting school. These young people are "drop outs" from life. It is difficult to explain why so many young people are unsuccessful in negotiating the passage from teen years to the adventure of adult life. Some get lost in the disabling effects of long term substance abuse. Others seem to be engulfed in the world of video games.

I worked for three years with a 60 year old woman who was recovering from a serious depression. She had been a very successful administrator in a federal agency but had retired because of her disabling illness. Her inability to reestablish and maintain a healthy emotional state involved her 28 year old son. He had graduated from college in a technical field that was much in demand. Instead of looking for a job and planning to live on his own, he remained at home and gradually fell into a routine that caused his parents endless aggravation. He slept almost all day, arose in the late afternoon, had something to eat alone, and then retired to the basement recreation room where he played video games until early morning when he would have another meal and then go to bed. Occasionally on a Saturday he would invite two or three young men he knew from college to come and play games throughout the night.

His mother was willing to put pressure on him to get a job and to move out of the home, but the father, who came in for two or three joint sessions, was unwilling to consider it. The issue was never resolved while I was still seeing her. For all I know it may remain a stalemate. It is interesting to note that when I visited Russia two years ago as a delegate of the American Psychiatric Association, the psychiatrists at one of their major hospitals spoke about their program for "computer addiction." I have not heard of similar programs in the United States, but I have seen many individuals between the ages of 15 and 40 who would probably fit criteria for such an addiction.

Other young adults seem to be fulfilling some vague and unspoken family role that keeps them from having a life of their own. Parents are often labeled as "toxic" to their children, and Susan Forward, Ph.D. has provided many examples in her book "Toxic Parents" (Bantam Books, N.Y. 1989). The fathers and mothers of these stay-at-home adults would deny any intention or desire to have this son or daughter continue living with them. But the offspring may feel "needed at home" by a parent who denies an alcohol problem, by parents who have planned to divorce "when the children are all gone," by a parent who is emotionally or physically abused by the spouse, or by a parent who is emotionally dependent on them. These young people often seem bland and without much feeling. They show little or no enthusiasm for things. They avoid other people so anger is rare. Their attachment to others appears to be lacking, and without attachments one does not encounter loss and consequent sadness. Their sheltered existence evokes minimal anxiety. However, if their way of life is threatened, they may then react with fear, anger, and even violence. I have talked with several parents who maintain the status quo for this very reason.

Some young adults continue at home because a father or a mother chipped away at their self-confidence through the years and gradually undermined the enthusiasm and ambition that was naturally theirs. Confidence in oneself is a fragile attribute in the young whether age 14 or 34. Even older adults know how easily a positive attitude about one's own abilities can be shaken by an employer, a peer, a spouse, or an elderly parent. Did you ever tell a funny story, and no one laughed? Did you ever plan an event for someone, and the person never commented? Have you taken up a cause at a meeting and suddenly realized that no one else is supporting it? Didn't you doubt, at least for a moment, whether or not the story was funny, whether or not the event was a success, whether or not the cause was worthwhile? Suppose for years no one ever laughed at funny stories you told or never responded to sad or unpleasant experiences you talked about. Suppose for years no one ever acknowledged any of the positive things you did. It is always distressing to work with an adult whose family never commented on good report cards, good behaviors, special ability in art or music or sports. A struggling adult once told me, "I never had anyone tell me I was worthwhile." These individuals seem to have a void in their life that is inaccessible to positive experiences of their own or affirming comments of others. There is something frozen deep inside them, left by the chill of parental coldness.

I have often encouraged patients to think about emotions the way they might think about money. People are generally more careful about what happens to their money than they are about what happens to their feelings. They know that they must have money available to buy the things they need on a daily basis. They know that if they invest they should invest well so that they will get some interest in return. They are also aware that it is a good thing to give to charitable endeavors. It is useful to think of emotions in a similar way. We need to use some of our emotional reserves to nurture ourselves and to reduce feelings of sadness, loneliness, and anxiety. When we invest emotionally in other people, it is important to take stock as to whether or not we are getting any return for our investment. This may sound a bit self-centered, like "don't be nice to others unless they are nice to you." However, it can be wasteful to lavish love on someone who demonstrates no affection in return.

There is a difference between charitable acts and loving acts. Being kind to someone and doing nice things for that person does not require an expenditure of feelings. It is not unusual for an adult child to be in a position of caring for or visiting an aging parent toward whom they feel a deep resentment because of their own neglected or abused childhood. In such a situation, the caretaker may often have a sense of guilt because he or she dislikes the obligatory behavior and even feels hypocritical in providing care when there is no love to go with it. Acts of charity and kindness toward others whether they are family members or strangers are not diminished if they are performed without a positive emotional component. If there is no love involved, it is very much like donating money to charity; it is a good thing to do, and love is not a prerequisite.

A more telling situation occurs when one party in a relationship ceases to respond in any meaningful way to the affection and devotion of the other party. It is difficult for the loving individual to maintain an investment of affection indefinitely with no return. If there is no possibility of improving the relationship, the likely choices are to withdraw the investment or eventually to become emotionally depleted (bankrupt), resulting in depression.

Anger is certainly a significant emotion which we face in our pressured world. One of the most subtle sources of our displeasure in life comes from our frustrated desires. In the chapter on children we noted that children become angry when they cannot do things, when they cannot have things, or when they are separated from mother before they are ready. The period of adolescence provides a time of learning to accept limits imposed by authority figures and by life events. The lesson is never completely mastered or completely accepted. We go through life wanting, deep inside, to have things go the way we want them to go and to have what we want to have. I believe that the resultant frustration with the realities of life is a contributing source of the unprovoked, seemingly spontaneous, and random violence sometimes seen in adults.

Road rage is an example of the adult who harbors a resentment that goes far beyond the other driver who got in the way. Someone else has been "in the way" before this incident. Individuals who feel deprived of the things that advertisers tell them they should possess, who are unable to accommodate to their own limitations, who want relationships they have been unable to find, for these reasons or a number of others may feel abused and easily become enraged. Some insignificant incident lights the fuse. It might be the critical comment of a supervisor, an offensive remark by a peer, or an extended stare by a passer-by. The explosion follows.

Persons who have experienced abuse of any kind as children are prone to anger as adults, and their anger is likely to imitate that expressed toward them when they were young. Parents who were belittled in their youth tend to be hypercritical of their children. Adults who were physically abused as children are more likely than others to abuse their own offspring. Grown-ups who were sexually abused when young are inclined to sexually abuse their own or other children. The reasons for these behaviors are complex and not fully understood. We know that people who are victimized sometimes come to the point of identifying with their persecutors. The motivation for this is related to a desire to turn a frightening situation into something less traumatizing and to see the attacker in a better light. Over time the victim can accept the situation as justified. I have often heard patients justify the abuse they experienced as children by making excuses for the abuser. "My father only did what he had to do to straighten me out." "My mother beat me only when it was necessary." The female victim of incest may say, "My father was so lonely, and my mother was such a shrew."

John, a 56 year old veteran of the Korean Conflict, became a patient of mine some 20 years ago. He came to the office with his wife who stated that his anger was getting "out of hand." John was by far the angriest patient I have ever treated. He was perpetually so, unapologetically so. Interviews were filled with torrents of offensive language. During the first several months of therapy I had a difficult time piecing together a reasonable case history because during each visit he seemed to need to use all the profanity and foul language at his command. He had worked at a major retail store in the Midwest prior to entering the navy during the Korean Conflict. He had a previous marriage with no children. It ended badly, but he never gave any details. He had a brother somewhere with whom he had no contact. His parents were deceased, and I obtained very little information about them or about his childhood. His ship had served in hostile waters during the war. Shortly after his discharge he married a woman 15 years his senior. John had a 20% disability from the Veterans Administration relating to his service. He would never discuss the basis of the disability, but I assumed it to be psychological. He had a collection of guns at home, and once each week he would go target shooting with another veteran. As he described these events he would become quite animated and would identify the targets as individuals he had known.

While he was my patient the Veterans Administration sent him a letter stating that his disability was going to be reduced from 20% to 15%. His anger became focused on the state V.A. headquarters, and he reported fantasies of going there with several of his guns and shooting people. He gave me permission to write to the V.A. which I did. Fortunately my letter impressed them sufficiently, and his disability payments were left intact. His response made me feel like I had saved his life. Perhaps my letter saved the lives of others. Soon after all of this was resolved I moved to another city. It was impractical for him to consider continuing treatment with me, but he insisted on doing so. John and his wife would make the six hour trip each month. I would see him the evening of his arrival and again the next morning before he left to return home. Both sessions were used to air old grievances in the same colorful language. This continued for about one year. Then he had a heart attack, and he felt unable to make the trip. He would call every two or three weeks, and we would talk for 15 or 20 minutes. The last time we talked he reported that the doctors had recommended heart surgery, but he opposed the procedure. His physical condition and his psychological stability were tenuous. I did not question his decision. A few weeks later I had a call from his widow. She had been shopping one day and on return found him dead. It was a peaceful end for a man whose violence had been precariously contained.

There is another story about John that shows a different side of this man. Before I moved to my new location I was doing psychiatric evaluations for the Social Security Administration. One day when John was leaving after his regular appointment, a man was waiting alone in the reception room. There was no office person in the area. The man was unkempt, with long hair and unshaven, and wearing tattered clothes. He was there for a disability assessment. As John departed I invited the man into my office and began the interview. A few minutes later there was a knock on my office door. I opened it and saw John who said very quietly, "Are you alright?" I assured him I was safe, and he left. John's anger was controlled in other settings, and it was released in the tirades which we called therapy. That release, that safe sanctum was all that I could offer him. On the positive side, he could live his wrath for that hour with me and find acceptance for who he was and for the terrible things he felt and thought about doing. He could then go about his life in a manner that was gentle with others.

Many angry adults are not open about these feelings because they are either not aware of them or not willing to talk about them. They are prone to express them in certain behaviors or, as therapists say, "act them out." Their displeasure shows in caustic remarks, teasing comments, or disparaging statements which they deny were meant to be hurtful when the target person is offended. It is a sort of "hit and run" technique. Parents sometimes use it with their children, spouses with one another. It acts as a ploy which provokes the recipient to show some irritation. The originator can then accuse the other person of starting any quarrel which ensues. Others do not limit their fury to nasty comments. They become loud and accusatory using obscenities to expose the force of their feelings. Regrettably there are an increasing number of angry people who do not limit their rage to verbal expression but move into physical assault all too readily. Police reports disclose disquieting data about the seriousness and frequency of this behavior.

Individuals also "act out" their anger in ways that are not physically aggressive but which are none the less hurtful to others. An angry spouse comes home intoxicated or stays out all night. One of a couple fails to do tasks agreed on such as cooking dinner or doing the laundry. One partner has an affair. Acting out one's wrath can involve minor situations such as shared chores or major situations such as infidelity. Angry words cannot be taken back, but they can be forgiven with apologies and forgotten over time. Physical assault can sometimes be forgiven with expressed regret, but it is not easily forgotten and should not be because there looms the strong possibility that it will happen again. Some acting out of anger is easy to pardon when everyone has calmed down, but rage that results in a serious breach of the relationship may not be reparable without some outside intervention over a period of time.

As we speak of forgiveness it is important to clarify some issues. Individuals often ask, "If I forgive someone, do we need to be friends again?" People often confuse forgiveness and reconciliation or bind the two together as part of the same action. Church goers hear the story of the prodigal son as a story of the father pardoning his errant son. I believe it is a story of reconciliation between father and son because the father had forgiven him long before he saw him coming, "still a long way off." Those words suggest a picture of the father standing on a high place and searching the horizon hoping to see his son coming home. Even if the son never returned, I believe his father had absolved him. Absolving another does not require restoration of harmony. Continued forgiveness may be more readily maintained by avoiding the offender. In fact, severing contact may be the wiser choice. People sometimes say, "I try to forgive him for what he did, but I still get angry when I think about it." Forgiveness is an intellectual act, a decision one makes about a past hurt done by another. It is a choice to pardon the person who did the injury, but it does not repair the damage. Memory of the event brings back the feeling associated with it and reawakens the anger, and when the irritation is revived the act of forgiveness seems less clear.

A particular area of violence should be mentioned, namely, the violence relating to sexual behaviors and primarily to the sexual violence of men toward women. Rape is the most heinous example. There are other examples of assaults on women that are not so obvious. Attitudes that set women up as objects for the satisfaction of male desires, to be used or abused, are degrading, and although there may be no physical attack involved, there is emotional violation. If one espouses the position that sexual behavior is solely a physical act, somewhat like defecation or urination, devoid of any emotional component, then the comments above are overstated. But if one accepts the premise that sexual intimacy naturally embraces an emotional component and is more than a simple biological act, the question that must then be asked is, "What is that emotional component?"

Do you remember past comments about attachment? The physical embrace of mother and child was the beginning of attachment and far more than just mechanical contact. The attachment needs of adolescents brought them into contact with peers and when combined with sexual urges developed into youthful love for special persons. It is difficult to doubt the presence and the value of this need for bonding in humans. We see it in mature adults and in the elderly for whom physical intimacy provides a continuing connection that strengthens the desire to love ever more deeply and spiritually. Sexual intimacy is a natural component of certain adult bonding behaviors. Sexual intimacy without desire or inclination for attachment is more bondage than bonding.

There are many ways of expressing irritation. Silence is one of the least recognized but most troublesome methods of showing displeasure. When we interact with other people it is natural to have expectations about how they will respond to what we say or what we do. If we say something or do something expecting a response and there is none, then we are left with the need to fill in the blank. If you have agreed to go shopping with your partner and you are thinking of changing your mind, you might say, "I'm not sure I want to go with you." If your partner does not reply, you are left to decide what she or he must be thinking and invariably it is not going to be positive, especially if you didn't think your comment would be well received. If you catch your 14 year old daughter sneaking in at two o'clock in the morning and you say nothing other than "Goodnight," you can imagine how she will lay awake wondering what you were thinking. Silence of the mad person can be maddening for others. I have had a number of teenagers tell me how devastating the tacit parent can be.

It is not the healthiest technique for either party. Unspoken anger often grows and during the waiting time may find harsher words when finally expressed. And the person who is waiting may find sterner words for self than the angry person will eventually speak. If an individual is furious and responds immediately with some cruel words, the recipient of the wrath may find it easier to forgive and forget what was said during the unreasonableness of rage. The Bible (Ephesians 4:26) says, "Do not let the sun go down while you are still angry." I take that to mean, "Get over it today, settle it now."

I saw a 42 year old corporate executive as a patient several years ago. Tom came to see me with complaints of insomnia and explained that he had recently undergone some minor surgery for sinus problems. After the surgery he had been given narcotics for pain, tranquilizers for anxiety, and sedatives for sleep. His physician was reluctant to continue the medicines without a psychiatric evaluation. Tom spent considerable time during the first interview explaining to me how prominent, how wealthy, and how influential his parents were in his home state. He was married and had three young children. His wife was a successful realtor. Two issues were clear from the initial interview. First, he was concerned that his pills be continued, and second, he wanted others to think well of him (perhaps because he did not really think well of himself). Both items became a focus of therapy. His internist had weaned him off the narcotics. He expressed acceptance of my detailed time table to taper and eventually discontinue the anxiety pills and sleeping pills.

His need for approval seemed more like a need for admiration. He was obvious and almost childlike in his efforts to impress me. He initially told me that his mother who died the previous year was a psychiatrist, and he spoke of her as being quite prominent in her work. Later I learned that she had been a career counselor. His father was deceased eight years. He spoke of him with great admiration for his political influence and his accumulation of wealth. Later I learned that he had lost a great deal of his money gambling and had seriously abused alcohol. He recounted his own successful Ivy League college years and his prowess on the football field. Later I discovered that football was played in high school, and he was not as successful there as his younger brother had been. He also came to acknowledge that grades had been a major problem in college because of his alcohol and drug abuse.

In his fourth year of college he cheated on his regular girl friend, and she dropped him. In retaliation he overdosed on alcohol and cocaine and then cut his wrist superficially. His father came and took him home for about ten days. There was no medical intervention because there was an unwritten code of secrecy in the family regarding any untoward behaviors. In fact, the incident was never discussed within the family. This pall of silence kept anyone from confronting Tom's dangerous and destructive behaviors as well as those of his father and his two siblings. He described his mother as unemotional. He always tried to please her but was never sure that he did so. His father was "absent a lot." Tom always wondered how his parents felt about him. They never expressed anger toward him, disappointment in him, or concern for him. He grew up with a disturbing picture of himself, knowing his faults and failures but unwilling to let anyone else know their extent or how much they frightened him.

After a few initial visits Tom brought his wife in for one meeting at her request. He was irritated when she revealed that he had been getting tranquilizers and sedatives on the internet from foreign sources. I made it very clear that the medicine schedule should be strictly adhered to and spelled out for both of them the number of pills to be taken each day for the next three weeks in order to terminate their use safely. He came in alone for two more visits, each time trying to defend the fact that he had been getting medicine from another source. After that he canceled a couple of appointments and then told me that he would be out of town for several weeks and would call me on return.

During that time his wife called me and said that he was drinking heavily, becoming very angry, and at times violent. He had signed an authorization for me to talk to his wife. However, she asked me not to reveal her conversation because she was afraid of him. He called and came in for another appointment. I told him I would continue to see him only if he would bring his wife on occasion at my request. (Because of his deception I considered it hazardous to treat him without a reliable source of information as to his behavior at home.) He agreed and made another appointment but canceled it within a few days. He never returned. Tom was a victim of the "quiet anger" of his parents. I sometimes wondered if he thought they didn't get angry at him because he wasn't worth it. Now that both were deceased he could only continue to face the doubts and fears associated with their silence.

Before leaving the topic of anger it might be appropriate to comment on its spread throughout the world. While greed and lust for power are major sources of world problems, we cannot overlook the world inflamed with hatred and fear of one group for another. When we were babies we were naturally afraid of anyone who was different. Remember the response of the baby to someone who looked different because of wearing glasses? School age children are warned about talking to or going anywhere with strangers. Teenagers are warned about friends or classmates who are different. The racial, ethnic, and religious prejudices of parents get passed on to their children. In the process of growing up, many people learn to fear and then to hate those who are different. Gang fights, riots, wars and genocide offend us all. But we seem able to justify the wars we fight, the racial divide that separates our communities, and the church driven bias that enters our politics.

Anxiety is another emotion that is prevalent in the lives of adults. People live at a higher level of apprehension in our present society than they did several decades ago. The information age brings frightening scenes into our living rooms. News of world disasters is at our doorstep. Methods of travel are faster, more worrisome, and more dangerous. Communication is more available and more demanding. Inflation, the national debt, global warming, political corruption, and the threat of terrorists are among the many items that make people ill at ease. These concerns affect everyone and provide an inescapable background for the every day cares of living.

There are also personal items that lead to disquietude. Television talk shows and "House Call" medical programs as well as newspaper and magazine articles provide information which can cause anxious persons to develop health concerns that are completely unfounded. Those who are troubled about their physical appearance spend large sums of money for plastic surgery which may improve their body shape but rarely reduces their distress for very long. Those who worry about their social skills and their interpersonal relationships read self-help books and learn some catchy platitudes which fade quickly with time.

Earlier we touched on the fact that people often develop anger when they cannot have what they want. That seems to be the end point of unreachable goals and unachievable desires. But the effort expended along the way trying to attain those goals and fulfill those desires causes tension. Many adults are highly competitive and measure their success in life by comparisons to what other people have or are able to do. Large homes, expensive cars, exotic travel become essential items to allay any misgivings they may have about themselves and their accomplishments. Leisure, relaxation, quiet, and calm are not priorities in their hectic race to get ahead of one another.

Obviously one of the most important factors in the lives of adults is the work they do. Regrettably the job has become a source of stress for many. Small companies have been bought up by corporations which may in turn be taken over by larger firms. Down-sizing results in loss of employment for many, or even if it does not occur, rumors float around for months or even years suggesting it might happen. The job market changes rapidly because of new technology, and many people have difficulty keeping up with the changes. Many large companies are adding tests to their hiring process, and these may intimidate job seekers. Older individuals are less likely to get hired in many fields, and "older" may begin in the late 40's. Sometimes to remain employed one must agree to move to another area of the country. One of the common problems seen in the psychiatrist's office these days involves work related anxiety and depression. Companies expect more work and longer hours for the same compensation. In the past several years I have seen many patients who could not keep up with their work load unless they stayed late in the evening or came in on the weekend and sometimes both. Other employees had been terminated or retired, and the work had been spread out among those who remained. These longer hours at work made it difficult to keep up with their obligations at home. The piece that is always sacrificed first is recreation and relaxation time. The workplace has become a truly unfriendly place for many.

Those in professions do not escape work pressures. Lawyers in large firms are required to have a certain number of "billable hours," and these are sometimes charted so comparisons can be made by everyone. Since they are presumed to be mature individuals, do you think that posting productivity would create anxiety for them? It certainly did for the four or five I saw over the past few years. Physicians certainly have their stress filled situations. Advances in medicine are occurring rapidly, and conscientious doctors need to keep current with new medicines and new treatments to provide the best care for their patients. Malpractice lawsuits are always a possibility even when the care rendered meets the highest standards.

We spoke of curiosity in children and in adolescents as being a driving force in their lives. The same is true of adults. We desire to know why people do things that are unusual or bizarre. We want to know about the private lives of celebrities, about clandestine activities of the government, about "never before revealed" views of history. A glance at the tabloids in the grocery store is convincing evidence of the popularity of "behind the scenes information." Behavioral scientists report that secrets are easily remembered information although not easily kept. On the one hand, we seem to be everlastingly curious about the lives of others, but, on the other hand, we are uneasy about the government's assumed need to pry into our private lives. This inquisitive nature of ours is undoubtedly a driving force behind inventions, exploration, and discoveries in the realm of science. These in turn have led to advances in health care, transportation, communication, and many other fields.

Although curiosity continues to appear as a significant motivating factor in the behavior of individuals across the life span, it is not commonly referred to as an emotion. This leaves us with the question, "What emotion is involved in curiosity?" I believe it is attachment or love. Among the Thomistic philosophers, love is referred to as an appetitive emotion because in loving we desire to possess or be united with the object of our love. Thomists wrote of the love of truth, beauty, and goodness. We speak of the love of learning, of discovery. That is precisely what curiosity is. It expands our world from the time we are infants by bringing us into contact with people and things and places that occupy our thoughts and our feelings as we encounter them and afterwards leave their traces in our memories.

This desire to know expands to become a desire to do, to explore, and to experience. Curiosity is the driving force behind many of the good things that happen in the world and has motivated individuals to reach for the stars, to plumb the oceans, and to dismember matter. I have a friend who is involved in the field of nanotechnology. When he talks about it his eyes seem brighter, his face lights up, his words come more rapidly. His enthusiasm is like that of a small child who has just been given the toy he always wanted.

Another friend recently introduced me to this same thirst for learning and discovery in the music world. David Wasser is an excellent concert pianist. When I attended one of his concerts,

I was very taken by the feelings expressed in the music, and as I listened I kept wondering, "Where does the feeling come from and how does it get to his fingers?" I asked him my question after the concert, and recently he was good enough to sit down with me for an hour and talk about it. He practices the notes so often that his fingers "know the music." They run through the music almost automatically "leaving my brain free," as he says, to listen for the anticipated sound of the next note and to adjust the subsequent note accordingly. The feeling expressed in the composition is David's area of search and discovery. He studies the music to find the emotion the composer had in writing it, and then he brings that emotion to his performance. During the fascinating discussion he made a very pertinent comment, "When I'm playing, I need to control my emotions. I need to be able to think." There is great value in that statement. He acknowledges that if he is too swayed by feelings, he will not be able to maintain the clear thinking he needs to perform well. After hours of practice to the point of perfection, after time spent connecting with the passion of the composer, it is his thought and judgment that must control every aspect of the rendition. He said something else which is pertinent to our topic. I asked what his reaction was to audience comments after the performance. Was he eager to hear whether or not they liked the concert? He replied that he does not depend on their comments to evaluate what he has done. As he is playing he knows whether or not it is well executed. I am indebted to David for my music enrichment and an excellent example of a fine mind at work.

His latter comment has some relevance for therapists. In teaching students I try to bring them to at least a beginning ability to evaluate their own work product as good or not good. The test of their therapeutic skill is within the hour and not with the eventual outcome of therapy. As the session is proceeding they need to be able to assess whether or not they are doing well. There will not always be a teacher or a supervisor to provide a critique.

There are, of course, instances of perverted love in the world such as love of money and of power. Greed is surely a corruption of a natural desire. To want things, to enjoy nice things is a normal feeling. But the appetite for things can become insatiable, and the good of others can be lost in the accumulation of wealth. Corporate crime provides many examples of this perversion. In some individuals the thirst for power falls into this category of love turned perverse because the eagerness to take control dominates their lives. They crave having influence and prestige. Anger often becomes a companion emotion in those who have authority over others. Being in charge of things can be a heady experience. Individuals who are good team players may change markedly when they are promoted to supervisory positions. When others are expected to do our bidding it is a short step to feeling displeased when they do not. Despots are likely to treat others like chattel.

In the first paragraph of this chapter we borrowed from the dictionary and referred to the adventure of adulthood as a daring and exciting activity. Some adults crave high excitement and appear to become addicted to it. They move on the fast track of life, searching for thrills of whatever kind they can find, never fully satisfied with the last and always anticipating the next. The ambition to discover new experiences may overshadow good judgment and consequences can be dangerous. A few people find sensational experiences in diverse ways. Some have work that is exciting, and others find stimulation in their recreational pursuits. Most adults have routine lives and are not aware of much that is adventurous or absorbing in their day to day existence. They find their excitement in watching movies or television. Perhaps the most daring thing they do is drive in heavy traffic.

Is it possible that we have lost our ability to enjoy the people and the events of our personal lives because we are so caught up in what we watch in the movies and on television? Do we live so vicariously through the actors that when they portray an enjoyable time we think we have had one too? If we have a desire for some excitement, is it satisfied by a couple of hours of Law and Order? Are our feelings of anxiety and awkwardness in social situations increased by watching movies and TV shows in which everyone always knows exactly what to say and what to do? Do we envy the ease with which TV guests respond so adroitly to interviewers? Do we sometimes wish that we could tell everyone about something in our personal life? I recently heard Paula Zahn say to someone she had interviewed on television for about 15 minutes, "Thank you for this private conversation with me tonight." It was as private as all the personal revelations that are voiced unabashedly on the regular talk shows. The virtual intimacy captivates our attention and pours pictures and sounds into our brains. The sensory input from the screen makes us laugh, frightens us, makes us cry, cheers us up, and at times, makes us envious. The resultant feelings are about as real as the pictures on the screen and about as lasting. When we turn the television off, they are gone.

If adults want excitement in their lives, they need to look for it and find it in the ordinary events they encounter. I recently watched our 8 year old granddaughter's excitement as she sat and eagerly read a book her mother had just bought for her. Not long ago, I had a patient tell me about his design for a lamp to be made of wood and stained glass. His enthusiasm was obvious. Wouldn't it be more exciting and satisfying to tell your partner or a close friend those things you thought you might like to tell the whole world? Have you talked to prospective parents who almost can't wait for the baby to arrive? Some people are thrilled listening to music. What difference does it make if it's Pavarotti or Willie Nelson? It's their music. Remember in an earlier chapter when I mentioned taking a walk with a four year old? How can they be so enthralled by the sight of a tiny flower or the chirp of a single bird? The better question may be, "How is it that so many beautiful things in the world no longer get our attention, much less our rapture?"

A few years ago I was treating a 56 year old engineer for depression. With medication and therapy he was making a good recovery. It was reassuring to hear him talk about projects at work which he found absorbing and stimulating. One of the most fortunate things that can happen in life is to have a job that stirs us to do our best. Performing well at a task animates us and gives us a sense of accomplishment and even excitement. I saw a 65 year old patient who had retired at age 59 to take care of her bedridden mother. My patient had been a clerk in the same grocery store for 28 years. I believe she found it exciting to greet the same people over the years of waiting on them and to meet new customers as they found their way around. Many of them still called her and sent her greeting cards from time to time. She was warm, friendly, and cheerful in spite of the difficult situation that confronted her daily. She also had a great sense of humor. When I'm teaching students I let them know that I have found therapy to be not only a challenging field but also an exciting profession.

Individuals sometimes seem more connected to their favorite newscaster, actor, or athlete than they are to their spouse, their parents, or their friends. That sort of artificial bonding is certainly not demanding nor is it inspiring. And it will never be exciting. Is it too long ago to recall the passion you felt in those early weeks, months, and maybe years when you entered into a committed relationship with another? Has it grown cold? Or did it die? It might be useful to return to the comparison we made between emotions and money. If you invest large sums, you are either going to keep a check on how the investment is doing or you are going to pay someone else to do it. That makes good sense. If you entrust a great deal of your emotional well being into the hands of another person, you ought to pay attention to the ongoing health and stability of the connection you made. That too makes good sense. Persons who enter relationships of this kind too often have the expectation that the investment phase is over, and they can now expect perpetual returns.

Couple relationships seem to be difficult to maintain in today's world. The divorce rate continues to climb, and infidelity is a blight affecting marriage. All that has been written in this chapter about anger, anxiety, curiosity, and love was primarily focused on individuals. These emotions are present in all couple relationships but in a double dose. When two people are experiencing situations which create similar emotional responses in each of them, the effect is likely to be synergetic, producing a return even greater than the sum of their two individual reactions. If you and your partner are angry at each other, the anger of one fans the flame of the other's anger, which in turn feeds the wrath of the first. So a small argument can become a conflagration in a very short time. Books on saving your relationship agree that there is a need to talk openly about feelings with one another.

For most adults, talking about feelings does not seem to come naturally. Although I usually avoid suggesting differences between female and male behavior, I believe this is one area in which there are dissimilar patterns. Men do not easily show their emotions, and they have difficulty expressing them verbally. As a result, they are likely to retreat into silence when dealing with strong feelings. Women tend to be more demonstrative and more ready to talk about how they feel. The women's anger is increased by the man's silence, and the man's anger is increased by the demand that he find words for his feelings. Synergetic wrath is the result. It is important that wives and husbands appreciate differences of this kind so each one can try to make some accommodation to the other's attitude. However, when a person is highly irritated he or she is more caught up in "how I feel" than in what another's point of view might be. Talking things out is a great idea when it works. It is more certain to work when both individuals are calm, reasonable, and sincere.

There are several advantages coming from open exchanges between partners. Talking about one's day provides release from the pressure of emotional experiences. Discussion with a trusted person broadens one's perspective. We know that seeing with two eyes gives an individual perception of depth. You may recall looking at a two dimensional picture through a stereoscope and being surprised that the picture appears to have depth because there are two slightly different views of it. A frequently unrecognized benefit of a partner relationship is that it provides a stereoscopic view of life. No matter how close they may be, each person sees things a bit differently. That difference can expand their view and deepen their understanding. Another benefit from regular communication between partners is the enhancement of their attachment to one another as they grow deeper in their knowledge of each other.

Several articles and books have appeared lately providing statistics and information about the baby boomers, that group born during the 20 years following the end of the World War II in 1946. Their transition to second careers has been noted in a survey done by the American Association of Retired Persons (AARP). The February 20, 2006 issue of Newsweek contained a lengthy article by Barbara Kantrowitz quoting data from an AARP survey of the sexual behaviors of this age group. I did not quote statistics in discussing adolescence nor will I discuss the specifics of the above article. There is a vast difference between the available figures relating to sexual conduct and the emotional fall-out from those behaviors. The numbers become percentages of persons who engage in this or that behavior. They tell us nothing about the powerful feelings that can be associated with adult sexual behaviors and misbehaviors: feelings of love, betrayal, doubt, happiness, loneliness, jealousy, compassion, union, sadness, guilt, ecstasy, emptiness. Surveys can never explore, expose, or explain the depths of passion associated with sexual relationships.

The baby boomers have been a competitive group focused on what others had and what others were doing. Some teenagers feel they are missing out when they hear about or read about the percentages of youth who are using this or that drug or engaged in this or that sexual behavior. Many adults are no less likely to base some of their behavioral decisions on what other people are doing. Decisions can be difficult to make when a strong physiological attraction is involved. For a person who loves chocolate, it is not easy to sit in front of a piece of chocolate cake and forgo the pleasure. It would be even more difficult if the person just read an article stating that 43% of people eat at least one piece of chocolate cake each day. Suddenly a temptation turns into a deprivation. When a baby boomer with active sexual urges reads an article discussing the frequency of various sexual activities in that age group, it sets an expectation or a goal. Anything less suggests either unfair restriction or sexual inadequacy. We often have problems making choices that we know we should make but would like not to have to make. The fact that "everyone is doing it" or even if it's only 20% or even 12% gives strength to our desire to do it. How simple it becomes for a survey of thousands of people to provide permission and justification for one individual decision!

Articles about the boomer generation often refer to their preparation for their later years. That is precisely the direction we will take in the next chapter when we discuss major emotional factors faced by the elderly.

CHAPTER V
The Expectations of Elders

We began life when our mother's time of expecting was completed. In old age we face a number of expectations including the anticipation of death. The title of this chapter seems appropriate when we consider that most adults look forward to these days of retirement and leisure for a long time, and they have many presumptions regarding this final period of their lives. We will review some of the more significant emotional reactions that occur during this stage of life. We will also consider some of the things that others expect from the elderly.

The beginning of adolescence is set primarily by the physiological development which brings about pubertal changes. The transition to adulthood is established primarily by legal definition. We recognize that maturity of the adult requires more than a legal decree. Now there is this later stage of life that needs to be separated from our common perception of adult years, but it is not easy to delineate when this season begins or how it is divided from the previous time. This phase ultimately includes major physical, mental, and emotional changes and consequent alterations in life style. But none of these definitively mark the beginning of this period because they can occur much earlier in life. The onset of this portion of our existence has no clear distinguishing characteristics. Some see it as their retirement period, but this can begin as early as 50 or as late as 80. Persons who have worked 25 years for government agencies or large companies or who have been career military usually have good health benefits and a pension and may retire at an early age. However, many of them then decide to establish a second career. Other people, particularly in some of the professions, may continue working full time or part time into their 70's or even their 80's.

The Social Security Administration presently sets this transition at age 65 by providing full benefits then, although there is presently in effect a phased increase in the normal retirement age from 65 to 67. As a result, those born in 1960 or later will not qualify for full benefits until age 67. Some individuals look forward for years to the beginning of their social security payments but then find that part-time employment is necessary to supplement their monthly government check. Age 65 is not a firm line to define older age groups. AARP enrolls people at age 50 but that may be associated with enlarging their lobbying base as well as expanding their treasury. Senior centers post 55 plus for membership eligibility. Probably the majority of U.S. citizens would consider 65 as the breakpoint between adult and senior. After all of this discussion regarding the boundary between these two phases of life, for the purposes of this chapter I am going to consider the dividing age at about 75. Observing retirement facilities with provisions for long term care suggests that seniors in their mid 70's are often showing one or more signs of "getting old."

As people advance in years they experience limitations in some of their abilities, and for many it is this change, rather than their age, that tells them that they are moving into those "later years." The onset and the severity of this shift in function are extremely variable but nevertheless inevitable. Sensory acuity declines with obvious results. Eye glasses and hearing aids become more common. Glaucoma, cataracts, and macular degeneration are frequent medical problems. Hearing loss impairs social exchange unless auditory devices compensate. If hearing loss progresses to deafness, a sense of isolation develops. The sensitivity of taste, smell, and touch is also diminished with aging. However, there is some evidence that touch is less vulnerable and survives as the final avenue of communication when other senses are gone. In the first chapter we referred to proprioceptors, the organs of kinesthetic sense. These become less functional in oldsters and result in unsteady movements which are further complicated by decreasing muscle strength and arthritic changes. Falls are more common, bones are more fragile, and fractures are the result.

All of these sensory occurrences are not only conscious to the individual they are also apparent to relatives and friends. Other modifications in function are taking place which are not as obvious to others but which can be disconcerting to the senior. Memory loss is probably the most significant of these more subtle changes. If an elder mentions to a group of the same general age the fact that she or he has a memory problem, replies will be plentiful, "I can't remember anything either." They sometimes seem to compete with one another over who has the greatest memory loss. Not remembering names, forgetting where something was placed, overlooking birthdays and anniversaries are common problems. Older people often lose interest in current happenings and enthusiasm for various activities. Minor mood fluctuations occur during this same period.

Various health problems have their onset when the body's vitality is waning. Some of these become chronic problems such as diabetes, hypertension, and arthritis. Others require aggressive treatment and lengthy recovery periods such as cancer, stroke, and coronary artery disease. These also may leave behind lasting impairment. Health issues put an additional strain on the seasoned body as well as on emotional well-being. In fact, all of the items mentioned in the past several paragraphs combine to affect emotional life. Whatever adaptive powers the person had during earlier years will be called upon now in various ways and on frequent occasions. Individuals will cope with these problems according to the emotional resilience and repertoire available within them.

There is considerable validity in the saying that "as we become older we become more like ourselves." Past performance is the best predictor of what a person will do in the future. Those who have maintained a positive attitude in the face of various adversities in the past are likely to meet the vicissitudes of later years with equanimity. The ones who have fought with the troubling events of earlier times are likely to carry the same attitude into their retirement, and instead of the tranquility they expected they will remain as unsettled as before. Those who have been worriers will find that worry does not cease just because they no longer have to go to work or face the pressures of a daily schedule.

Seniors who have been in "the limelight" for one reason or another in the past may consider celebrity status important to their sense of well-being. If they excelled in their profession or their job and received a great deal of recognition, they may continue to seek compliments from others. In later years one finds them waiting for the opportunity to tell others about their many past successes. Elders whose former positions of power and prestige bolstered their egos may tend to seek positions of prominence among their peers. Individuals who have received public acclaim for their talent in music or in acting may find it difficult to bow out gracefully, and we see them performing poorly on stage or screen what they used to do so well. On occasion we see adults who behave as if they were assigned a particular role in life, for example, the "mother," the "prankster," the "beauty queen," the "clown." As they get older they cease to have the attributes that the role demands, and as a result, they have a difficult time fitting in with others because they no longer play the role well or their "audience" no longer provides the desired appreciation.

When I was practicing in a western state, a 72 year old widow came to my office referred by a prominent psychiatrist in the area. During the first visit she informed me that she had recently been to three other psychiatrists and found none of them to be helpful. She said that the person who referred her to me was a good friend of her deceased husband and herself. She felt certain that I would be of help. As she identified who she was, I realized that I had seen her at two or three large gatherings over the prior few years. I remembered her as an attractive woman who dressed well and seemed to draw considerable attention from others as she moved around the gathering. Now she looked more withered than one would expect at her age. Her clothes were more suitable for someone much younger, and her make-up seemed excessive and poorly applied. She complained of insomnia, anxiety, and loneliness. She said that the crowd of people she and her husband had associated with had died, moved away, or were unable to keep up with her energy. At the conclusion of her first visit, she insisted on seeing me at least once each week because "I know you are going to help me."

We met every week for about six weeks, exploring as much of her earlier life and her marital relationship as she was willing to discuss. She was her father's "princess" and an only child. Her parents had been prominent figures in the community. Her years in college were not scholastically remarkable but were "fun." She married shortly after graduation to a career soldier. She never revealed much about the depth or the parameters of the marital relationship. The couple had lots of friends with whom they enjoyed parties, traveling, and attending sports events. Her husband had been dead 18 months. Shortly after his death she had to move because the house "was too big to stay in alone." She seemed to mourn the loss of the house more than the loss of him. As we talked I found that her insomnia was not a significant problem and that her anxiety was related to her loneliness.

She seemed unable to come to grips with her social isolation other than to seek time in a psychiatrist's office. I suggested she contact old friends and try to reestablish some activities with them. I encouraged her to consider things she might do to discover new friends and expand her interests. The suggestions were ignored. After the first few weeks of therapy she began to request two sessions each week to which I would not agree. Later I began to raise some question about the limits of psychiatric intervention for her particular situation, commenting that the problem seemed to be more related to lack of social contact and activities. At the same time I expressed a willingness to continue seeing her but suggesting less frequent visits. After one or two additional sessions she left a voice message saying that she wanted to cancel her next appointment and would not be seeing me any more because I had "not been of any help." I thought her statement was reasonably accurate. My thought was that she still saw herself as a "beauty queen" and was disappointed in others when they did not see her in the same way.

It has been an enlightening experience for me to serve on several committees of retired persons. Although these were advisory groups, it became clear in one of them that a certain member took the position that his advice should be followed by the head of the program. When the manager did not accept his recommendations he resigned from the committee immediately. He had been a managing director in a national company for many years and undoubtedly had a great deal of expertise. I do not believe that he forgot the definition of advisory. It is more probable that he was having a difficult time adjusting to his loss of authority.

Another member of an advisory group seemed dedicated to having a consensus when things of importance were addressed. On one occasion when a particular decision could have affected 200 or more people, he insisted that common consent was necessary from the entire group before a recommendation could be made. Two years later when he had a position with some minor authority the concept of consensus lost all interest for him. As a result, he alienated those with whom he worked. He had been in charge of his own company prior to retirement and continued to see himself as a "take charge" person. On occasion one meets a veteran who was a career officer and who clings to the authority and the prestige of those years even though they are long gone. These are examples of the manner in which retirees attempt to postpone losses that come with the transition.

Those considered above are exceptions to the great majority of persons who enter their advanced years with a belief that this period will in many ways be a valuable and interesting extension of the past. In the previous chapter we associated curiosity with the emotion of love. Sometimes I wonder if we should not consider curiosity a virtue, since it plays such a significant role in a healthy life style. It is certainly an important motivating force that weaves through the tapestry of our years, creating new patterns as we pass through each phase. The curiosity of children is wide-eyed wonderment. In teenagers it is exploratory, expansive, and experiential. In adults it is deepening, enriching, and absorbing. In seniors curiosity is persistent, quiet, and focused. Certainly older individuals are not finished loving, although they are no longer as interested in expanding their sphere of love to include other persons and other interests. At this point their loves are well established.

We noted how curiosity provided the impetus for children and adolescents and adults to reach out and find people to love and things to desire. Old age is the time when our curiosity prompts us to learn more about the value and the goodness of spouse, family, and friends; to know more deeply the beauty of the world of nature, of art, of music, and of literature; and to acknowledge and accept the verity of this "one and only life cycle." We need also to note that curiosity brings children into dangerous situations, adolescents into hazardous bypaths, and adults into a number of life's sordid sectors. Seniors are not immune to their own misdirected desires being fed by the empty promises of charlatans and the enticing advertising of con artists.

It is characteristic of humans to anticipate the future. Since we were old enough to know that there is always a day after this day, we have been oriented toward "what happens next." That question does not disappear in later life and is hardly answered satisfactorily with "I don't know." But "I don't know" is far more reasonable than "I don't care" because the latter defies our curious nature to want to know, to care to know, to love to know. Prior to this phase of life tomorrow was always what happened next (except when it unexpectedly didn't for some). Now individuals know that tomorrows will end. Throughout our lives curiosity propelled our desire to seek goodness, beauty, and truth even when our depiction of those was far from accurate. With advancing age goodness continues to be found in significant relationships as well as in the casual warmth of the stranger. Beauty may be differently defined, but it is there in the faces of family and peers as well as in that portion of the world that is still available though sensory channels. The search for truth takes on a heightened significance as death approaches. For many it is faith that emboldens the trust they have in the future. Healthy minded seniors look on these final allotted years as gift, as opportunity, as treasure, and (for many) as transition.

Those who are advanced in years have new anxieties which can bring worrisome days and restless nights. Aches and pains call attention to their bodies and remind them of their increasing physical vulnerability. Talking about anxieties is usually helpful, and they are likely to talk to friends about their concerns. Unfortunately the other person may have had similar physical ailments or knows someone who did, and perhaps, the outcome was not favorable requiring lengthy treatment or surgery, possibly without success. Most symptoms can have a variety of causes and a variety of treatments. There is some similarity between one person's chest pain caused by a muscle strain and the neighbor's chest pain heralding a heart attack. The anxious person cannot distinguish between the two and may only find the chest pain worsening after hearing about the neighbor. Emergency room physicians report that a large percentage of the patients they see who fear they might be having a heart attack are, in fact, experiencing a severe anxiety episode.

Worries about physical health can be allayed by honest discussion with one's primary care physician. The assumption in that statement is that the personal doctor is willing to take the time to listen attentively, to order and explain tests (if any are needed), and to educate and reassure the patient regarding the symptoms. In these days of managed care, doctors are hard pressed not to watch the clock during interviews because they rarely get reimbursed for time spent talking. Only psychiatrists have that luxury. We have mentioned before that anxiety is contagious and spreads from one person to another. If we discuss our physical ills with our neighbors, we are likely to catch some of their worries about whatever problems they may be having. In addition, anxiety about our physical health is a bit like an infection because it easily spreads from one area of the body to another.

A 76 year old widow was referred to me by her internist for an evaluation and treatment. She had been living alone since the death of her husband some 20 years before. They had no children. After her husband had been dead several years she got in touch with a widower whom they had known. They established an ongoing relationship. He traveled from his town to visit her almost every weekend, staying two or three days. This pattern continued for about two years. Then he died rather suddenly six months before she came to my office the first time.

Although she was still grieving his death, she seemed more anxious than depressed. She had a number of physical complaints which were being treated by her primary care doctor but which she would enumerate each time we were together. These included headache, muscle spasms, insomnia, poor appetite, and frequent gastrointestinal distress. The last was the main focus of her concerns and was presented in detail each time I saw her. The report included the foods she did eat and those she didn't eat and the gastric responses she attributed to each item of her dietary intake. She also compared her symptoms with those of two or three of her friends, and they engaged in diagnosing one another and recommending medicine or diet based on their individual experiences. She was about 5 feet 2 inches tall and weighed less than 90 pounds. She was very offended when anyone mentioned how thin she was. She obviously obsessed a great deal about her eating and her weight, although there was no history of an earlier obsessive compulsive disorder.

I speculated that there were other reasons for this current fixation and rumination. She was very uncomfortable about any reference to age, disability, or death. When one of these was mentioned, her typical response was, "I had a grandmother who lived to be 105, and I want to live as long as she did." I believe her anxiety related not so much to the loss of her friend or her husband but to the loss of her own life at some unknown future date. That was a topic which could never be broached successfully in our sessions.

When bodily symptoms result from anxiety, they may or may not be related to actual physical ills. Continued tension may contribute to stomach and intestinal pathology and may also be involved in circulatory, respiratory, and other systemic problems. We speak of psychosomatic illness when there is definite physical pathology resulting primarily from emotional causes. At other times excessive concerns may not involve the development of real ailments even though they cause definite symptoms. We noted above that chest pain often occurs in a person who is apprehensive and hyperventilating. In this case the pain is not related to a physical problem. Anxiety of this sort sometimes migrates from one organ or body part to another.

Rosa came to see me because she was worried that she had interstitial cystitis, i.e., bladder inflammation and irritation. Her concern was based on a problem of frequent urination. She had seen two doctors, neither of whom had confirmed her belief. But she had researched urinary problems on the internet and based on her symptoms was convinced of the accuracy of her self-made diagnosis. However, she volunteered the comment that since she had moved to Maryland one year ago she had developed a number of physical complaints which seemed to come one after the other. She had experienced shoulder pain for several weeks, and when that was gone she developed a dry cough which also lasted several weeks. After that cleared up spontaneously she began having urinary frequency.

We spent several weeks discussing her family of origin and her current relationship with her husband and adult son. Rosa grew up in a Latin American country where the father was dominant in the home. He treated the children harshly at times, and she acknowledged that as a child she was frightened of him. She commented that she presently owed him filial respect but felt dislike for him. Her mother, who had been dead for two years, came from a wealthy family and had traveled a great deal during her married life, leaving her children with a nanny when they were young. Rosa's relationship with her husband had grown more distant, partly because of her focus on her physical ailments as they shifted from one part of her body to another. Issues with her father had not been resolved because she continued to be uneasy in any contact she had with him. We focused on this relationship, bringing it to a more comfortable level for her. She was encouraged to reestablish a more intimate connection with her husband. This was accomplished and brought her a sense of security. We also discussed bladder training and the association between anxiety and urinary frequency. Her physical symptoms improved rapidly as she lost her disquietude and continued to have easy communication with her father and improved ties with her husband.

The care-free life that oldsters anticipate can be disrupted by a variety of concerns. Financial security is frequently one of them. Pension plans are less secure. Those who depend on investments see large fluctuations in the stock market. Critics of Medicare question its solvency. The cost of living increases regularly and relentlessly. Reviewing one's financial position in terms of the future involves two questions. How much do I need? How long will I need it? One cannot answer the first question without having an answer to the second, and there is no clear answer to the second no matter at what age it is asked. Mortgages and loans have end points. We know how much we need and for how long to pay them off. Not so with retirement funds! Older people have two fiscal unknowns: how dependable is their income source and how long will they need it. Their anxiety shows in extensive coupon clipping, shopping only for sale prices, and sharply curtailing expenditures.

Conservative spending is always a prudent approach but turning miserly narrows our view of life by focusing our attention on money. The elderly are not usually prone to avarice unless they always were so. Individuals who have been level-headed and sagacious in financial matters are likely to maintain the same attitude in later years. Money has value for them because it provides them with what they need. Those who measure their own value by the amount of money they have accumulated will probably never have enough and are inclined to hate to part with whatever they do have. Their worth, financial as well as personal, is based on a number!

Fear and insecurity prey on the elderly at times. After the hardships and worries of a lifetime individuals have often learned to hide their emotional responses from others. Spouses who have a close relationship are likely to be aware if the partner is troubled. But this is not always true because wife and husband can become protective of one another especially as time grows short. One partner who is seriously ill may not wish to share health information with the other. I have seen spouses in their later years who had become the confidant of a grown son or daughter and had either promised or felt obliged not to tell certain things to their partner. The mother is usually the confidante and may harbor the secret of a daughter's illegitimate pregnancy and abortion, a son's gay relationship or gambling debts, a daughter's drug use, or a son's involvement in criminal activities. This arrangement places an unfair burden on the parent who holds the confidential information. In addition, it creates a barrier between the parents if they cannot be honest with one another. Furthermore, it can cause antipathy at a later time if the one finds out that the other concealed information on behalf of the adult child.

I saw a 72 year old woman whose 30 year old daughter was living at home with her and her husband. The daughter frequently invited a male friend from work to dinner with the family and to family gatherings. Her father either was told by the daughter or assumed that the man was single. He would occasionally comment to his wife about his regard for the man and his hope that the daughter might fall in love with him and get married. At the same time the daughter had disclosed to her mother that the man was married and had two children, that she was in love with him, and that they were involved in a sexually intimate relationship. This was a religious family and would probably be considered "old fashioned" by today's standards. My patient was quite distraught having this information and pretending all the time to her husband that things were as he thought them to be. One might think that the girl's father was being naïve and was hiding from the truth in refusing to ask for more information. That could be accurate, but that would not relieve the conflict between him and his wife that was inherent in the situation. It was an unfair request by the daughter, an inappropriate burden for the mother, and a subtle assault on the marriage bond. Perhaps one might add "an assault on two marriage bonds."

Persons who have weathered the turbulence of life with apparent composure have sometimes unknowingly reached the boundary of their emotional tolerance. Many years ago I was asked to provide a consultation for a hospitalized 75 year old woman. She was brought to the hospital by her son who had stopped by her house that morning and found her sitting staring into space and completely mute. When I saw her in the early evening she had been in the hospital since about 10AM and had not spoken or eaten. Various tests had been ordered and were in process with diagnostic concerns focused on a cerebral vascular accident. She lived alone since her husband died six months earlier. Her internist reported that she had been doing well since his death and that her general health was good. Her son informed hospital staff that she had been taking care of herself quite capably since the death of her spouse and was still driving, going shopping, and seeing friends.

When I entered her room there was no indication that she was aware of my presence even though her eyes were open. I introduced myself, told her that her internist had asked me to come to see her, and then I sat quietly by her bed. After a while I spoke to her again and said that I knew she could hear me and that I thought it must be frightening for her to be in the hospital and possibly not know what was going on. I explained that her son had brought her to the hospital earlier in the day, and I discussed the items in the chart that had been noted by her physician and the nurses.

I spoke softly to her and without any indication that time was important. I wanted her to understand what I was saying and be reassured by the care and concern of the hospital staff. After this I sat quietly for a short time and then asked if she would like to tell me if something had happened that day that had frightened her. She remained unresponsive for two or three minutes. Her first words were, "The water." Once we got through the wall of silence we went on together very slowly and very calmly to connect the pieces that caused this abrupt loss of function.

She and her husband were very attached to each other. He had been ill for nearly one year before his death. During the last six months of his life he was confined to his bed or a nearby chair, and she had provided the care he needed. He was opposed to having someone else come into the house as a part-time caregiver. Although her son and neighbors offered to help she insisted that she could manage on her own. In addition, her husband always seemed to become either anxious or angry when she was not readily available. She would rush to the grocery store and finish her shopping as quickly as possible so he would not be alone for long. She rarely talked to friends on the telephone because she was so attentive to his every need. Her son would come to visit, but she would encourage him to spend the time with his father. After her husband died she was terribly lonely, but she felt some relief and that caused her to feel guilty. She hurried to get back in touch with friends and to renew her prior schedule and interests. She rarely spoke about his death because talking about it only made her sad and rekindled the guilt she had experienced. She said, "I sometimes felt that I couldn't take anything more."

The morning that her son brought her to the hospital "something more" had happened. It was totally unrelated to other external events, but it was directly related to the dammed up feelings that had accumulated over the preceding 18 months: taking care of her husband, always rushing, always behind, feeling overwhelmed by his demands, waiting for him to die, watching him go, feeling relief and guilt, holding back her grief, and trying to contain and control all her feelings. The "something more" was a water pipe in her kitchen that broke and flooded the area before she could turn it off. It was the proverbial last straw. It was as if her brain was a pattern of pipes that became too full of pressure and shut off completely to keep from flooding her world with the rancid water of her pain and sorrow. We talked for an hour that evening and again the next day. I saw her the third day before she was discharged. She was in good spirits and by then had unburdened much of what had weighed so heavily on her heart for so long a time. It was one of those indelible and awesome encounters that I have been blessed to experience in my work.

We have referred to a number of physical and mental changes taking place which constitute losses for the elderly. Fortunately these usually occur gradually and thus allow the person time to accommodate to them. However, they do happen, and no matter how graciously they are accepted they are grieved by the individual. This grief is not the anguish of someone who mourns the sudden loss of a loved one. It is more the heartache of a person who daily visits a sick friend who is becoming progressively more incapacitated and knowing that there is little that can be done to arrest the process that is taking place. Many elderly individuals watch this deterioration in themselves as they note each day their declining health. Most seniors meet these gradual transformations in themselves and in their life style with the same healthy attitudes and emotional patterns they employed during previous periods of adversity, disappointment, or distress. They try to maintain healthy schedules of sleeping, eating, and exercise to slow any physical deterioration. They continue projects, hobbies, and interests from the past and sometimes develop new ones. They continue their interaction with others through social contacts and group activities. Many search out opportunities to volunteer and find these both invigorating and rewarding.

In spite of all this, they recognize the gradual decline in their physical stamina, their sensory keenness, their mental acuity, and their emotional steadiness. They slowly develop comradeship with these limitations and make whatever bargains they can with their aches and pains. They often find solace in the memories that bring them back to other times and other places. They gain courage from the knowledge that their lives have been of value to others whom they met along the journey, others who benefited in some small way from their kindness, their patience, their love, their humor, or just their smile. The grand things they did, the important people they knew, the illustrious careers they had, the windmills they conquered seem less important day by day.

Death is said to be the leveler for all. Old age fails to prepare some people for the fact that equality will truly be everyone's fate. There are those who seem to deny the process whereby we all come eventually to a few common denominators. Some always remain competitive, trying to overwhelm peers with their embellished tales of bygone prowess, prestige, or wealth. It is distressing to see elderly persons who are unable to recognize and be satisfied with their present value as human beings no matter how frail they are physically or how limited they may have become mentally. They should know that others can still see worth in who and what they are today and not just in what their past accomplishments might have been or what their offspring may someday bring to the world.

Children and grandchildren are part of the legacy of the elderly, and their lives can bring joy and satisfaction to parents in their advanced years. This bond between generations is usually a salutary connection providing love and support from young to old and encouragement and love from old to young. Sometimes it is more of a bind than a bond because it holds too tightly and demands too much. In some other cultures it is the solemn duty of the young to provide and care for the older generation. In those societies adults strive to find suitable work for their children with the understanding that in later years those children will be in a position to care for the aging parents. That is not a common expectation in the United States. Some oldsters place excessive and unnecessary claims on their adult children and then use guilt to punish any neglect. When this occurs, it is typically an extension of the kind of relationship the family always had.

As one might expect, it is not the senior member who comes for therapy but the junior member.

Frank was in his 60's when he came to see me because of his transvestite compulsions. He was married and had one child. His wife knew of his cross-dressing and threatened to get a divorce if he did not control his behavior. He had never been arrested but acknowledged taking chances that could have led to his arrest. He was a bank executive and a good provider for his family. He attended a church support group for his addiction and was faithful to the program. He traced his compulsion to the age of puberty when he recalled his mother wearing seductive clothing around the house. His father was relatively absent in his formative years and divorced the mother when Frank was in his mid-teens. During his early years he felt uneasy around his mother because of her revealing dress and because she was too demonstrative, always hugging him and kissing him on the lips to his embarrassment.

His mother was now in her late 80's, living in a retirement community where she had numerous friends. She had two other sons and one daughter, none of whom paid much attention to her even though they lived within an hour's drive from her. Frank had always been the one who did errands for her and who had taken care of the chores when she lived in her own house. He had power of attorney and managed her financial affairs. Currently he felt it was his obligation to take her to dinner once each week accompanied by his wife, who apparently had no fondness for her mother-in-law. He dreaded the event for four days beforehand and hated himself for doing it for the next three days. It seemed to be an inescapable burden for him. In our discussions he came to understand that his mother's influence on his compulsions persisted as a result of his servile behavior. He continued to do the other things that kept his transvestism under control, but he could not refuse his mother's expectations.

The harsh demands by elderly parents are problem enough while they remain alive, but the damage they cause often extends on after their death. Eleanor was an older patient referred by a local internist. She was an intelligent, personable, and friendly woman. She had incurred a number of losses in her life and seemed unable to meet the challenge of any of them. After 14 years of marriage her husband left her and their two children for a younger woman. She was terribly hurt and angry over his betrayal but dealt with the divorce in a passive manner. Eleanor had worked for a defense agency for 18 years and received consistently positive performance ratings. Years ago when she returned from a scheduled two week vacation she was told that she no longer had a job. Apparently the agency never gave her any explanation of what had happened, possibly because she never asked.

She was now living in her own house with a man whom she had been with for 15 years. He often drank and was verbally abusive to her. She was usually quite passive in these episodes but on occasion would strike back at him with a hurtful and threatening tirade. She never considered asking him to leave nor did she ask him why he never proposed marriage. She was constantly irritated by his unwillingness to let her know his work schedule and when she could expect him to be home. Their relationship was far from satisfactory, but she was never willing to look at what she might do to change it. She worked part time in a small business for very low pay considering her qualifications. Her employer would take advantage of her willingness to do tasks that were not part of her job and ask her to come in at unusual times.

Her history provided an understanding of her submissiveness. She had one brother, two years her junior. He had been very ill at birth and attention was focused on his survival. As he grew older the parents continued to dote on him. He won their approval on all counts. He was good looking, athletic, a good student, and popular. Eleanor was charged with being his protector at school and that seemed to be her only source of parental recognition. She had continued living at home through college years as her brother had done. Her father was particularly intrusive into her private life until she finally left home at age 23. Prior to leaving home, when she went out in the evening she was told when to be home, and when a man came to pick her up she had to introduce him to her parents. After a date she was always quizzed as to where they went, what they did, and whom they saw. One evening her father saw her in front of the house kissing her friend. He questioned her at length, and his comments left her feeling "cheap and dirty." Her brother became a successful attorney and moved to another state after his marriage. After his departure her parents looked increasingly to her to do minor errands for them when they were not feeling well or were pressed for time.

After Eleanor was married and had two children, she and her husband lived three blocks from her parents in a house her father had picked out, encouraged them to buy, and loaned them money to help them with the purchase. When the elders were in their late 70's, the mother became ill with a variety of physical complaints and a form of dementia. Eleanor's husband had left prior to this. The mother had frequent periods of severe pain and would become disoriented. The father would call Eleanor to come and quiet her or take her to the hospital if necessary. Eleanor slept with her clothes on for three years, anticipating the calls which more often came at night. Eventually her mother went to a nursing home and died there one year later. Her father had a heart attack about the time his wife went to the nursing home. He continued to live alone in the house until he died four years after his wife died. Eleanor was at his beck and call during that time too. The father could easily have afforded to pay for care in the home for his wife as well as for himself. His daughter was working and taking care of her two children on her own. The parents gave no recognition of her situation or her needs, only their own.

Therapists often take the position that patients have to stop the thoughts that seductively and destructively take them to the past. Patients need to "change their mind set," "stop playing the old tapes," or "leave the past behind." All of those are sound principles for moving on with our lives. But I have come to believe that some individuals have scars so deep and so damaging that no amount of therapy will bring healing, and no amount of remedial experiences will be curative. The psychic toxin Eleanor absorbed from her parents remained with her after their death, and I fear will remain with her until her death.

Seniors often compensate for the limitations of aging by talking about the accomplishments of their children and grandchildren. They tend to boast about the scholastic excellence of their offspring, their quick rise to positions of authority and high salaries, the size of their houses or cars, the trips they take, the brilliant and accomplished grandchildren they have produced. It is important for them to recognize the legacy of their lives, but if they have a need to stand on the qualifications of their progeny they appear to have lost some sense of their own worth.

We know that in some cultures the elderly are revered members of society and are valued for their wisdom and their counsel. They typically remain an integral part of the family unit until their death. This is rarely the case in the western world. Increasing numbers of aging persons are planning and preparing for the time when they will require assistance in their "activities of daily living," as the professionals call it. When such care is needed, it is difficult for daughters and sons with young families of their own to manage this care in their homes. Present day life is very busy with a great deal of coming and going on the part of family members. It is difficult to fit elderly parents into the active life of most households. Persons who plan ahead for their old age are often covered by long term care insurance policies, or they move into retirement facilities that have a full range of care. Life care facilities are an ideal situation for many old people. They support a continued sense of independence in a secure environment. They provide a broad range of social opportunities as well as a variety of activities. Most importantly they furnish levels of care extending from independent living to terminal nursing care.

When I studied experimental psychology many years ago, I learned the Weber-Fechner Law which states that our ability to observe increments of change depends on the percentage of change which occurs. If we add three ounces to a one pound weight, we can notice the difference between the pound weight and the one pound three ounce weight. If we add three ounces to a ten pound weight, we cannot distinguish the difference between the two because the relative amount of change is so small. Most oldsters who participate in activities, who enjoy reading or playing bridge or watching their favorite television shows, who keep in touch with family and friends, who have a hobby or volunteer somewhere, will say, "I can't believe the time goes so quickly. I never seem to have time to do all the things I want to do." Elders who remain involved are viewing the days and the weeks in proportion to the years they have lived. A week or a month is a very small increment of change for a person who has lived 80 or 90 years. It goes by so quickly one hardly notices it.

But when old people are focused on their losses and mark the lonely days, the hours of pain or discomfort, the sleepless periods at night, time goes by very slowly. Each day stands alone as the focus of their existence, separate from the 80 years that went before. If a pain filled day is not experienced with some relationship to a lifetime but only in the narrow perspective of the past painful days, then it looms larger and longer and passes more slowly. Those who complain endlessly about their aches and pains are often heard to say, "The day is so long and goes by so slowly. It seems endless." It is important to remain engaged in as much of life as possible for as long as possible, until it is "all gone."

I want to end this chapter with a quote from Francois Mauriac's "Cain, Where Is Your Brother?" (Coward-McCann, N.Y. 1962) "Old age is the sum of a life and each one of our acts, the least thought, is found in the end product."

CHAPTER VI

A Perspective on Psychiatry

This chapter will discuss some of the areas of psychiatric care which I have found to be of particular interest or special value. It will include comments about changes in the psychiatric profession, about complexities in therapeutic interactions, and about difficulties in diagnoses. I will discuss some of my personal views of the field of psychiatry and some of the limitations that I believe exist in providing good therapy. It will introduce two of my most interesting patients.

Psychiatry is a changing profession and would hardly be recognized today by pioneers such as Sigmund Freud, Alfred Adler, and Carl Jung who developed and brought attention to this new field of thought and of medical practice. Psychiatry was the "talking treatment" of the early 1900's, and psychiatrists practiced psychotherapy for most of the 20th century. There are two major factors that have altered the practice of psychiatry in the last 30 years. These are the advances in the field of psychopharmacology and major changes that have taken place in the health insurance industry.

It would date me to say that when I was a resident in psychiatric training there were only two or three antipsychotic medicines, no antidepressants, and some old fashioned sedatives available for use. Now the psychiatrist is deluged with choices of medicine for depression, mania, anxiety, sleep, psychotic symptoms, and some behavior problems. The use of these medicines can frequently improve the course of certain mental illnesses by favorably altering brain chemistry. The most obvious effect of medicine is the relief of symptoms, and when symptoms are lessened therapy can be more beneficial. Antidepressant medicine can increase the patient's desire to interact with friends and engage in activities, improve the sleep pattern, increase the patient's willingness to discuss problems and, of course, improve mood. Patients who are delusional and experiencing hallucinations have difficulty addressing life issues. After antipsychotic medicine diminishes the impact of these symptoms, patients can interact in a more coherent and reality based manner. Medicines for mania, anxiety, and OCD can also produce desired results when used appropriately.

With a wide range of studies showing benefit from these medicines, most psychiatrists have come to accept research findings indicating that a significant factor in mental illness is related to a change in brain chemistry. As a result, many believe that treatment consists primarily of finding the appropriate medicine to reestablish a salutary balance of these brain substances. There is no doubt that brain chemistry plays a major role in some emotional complaints, but there must be some explanation of what caused these particles to reach a state of disorder. Genetic factors play a predisposing role for many psychiatric maladies. But environment must not be overlooked. What happens in people's lives has an impact on their emotions. That is an inescapable truth. Symptoms of illness may be lessened with chemical remedies, but obsessive thoughts following a rape, depressive memories of childhood abuse, or distortions of reality based on repeated childhood trauma are not erased or resolved by pills.

Another factor which has shifted psychiatric emphasis from psychotherapy to prescribing medicines is the Managed Care Organization (MCO), which patients generally refer to as "my insurance company." One of the principal ways in which these organizations manage medicine is to determine who gets paid, how much, and for what services. Let me give an example from a payment schedule recently published by one of the nation's major Managed Care Organizations. For a session of individual therapy (45-50 minutes) by a psychiatrist, the MCO paid $90 less the co-pay, by a Ph.D. psychologist the MCO paid $70 less the co-pay, and by a Master's level clinician the MCO paid $60 less the co-pay. For a session of individual therapy (20-30) minutes, the MCO paid to providers, as listed above, $60, $40, and $35 respectively less the co-pay. The MCO also has a category called "medication management" for psychiatrists. This category includes a visit of 10 to15 minutes and is paid at a rate of $45 less co-pay. The mathematics of MCO management is simple. Based on the rates given above, a psychiatrist who does old fashioned therapy (50 minute sessions) can earn $90 per hour. A psychiatrist who just does medication management can earn $180 per hour for 15 minute sessions (each at $45) or $270 per hour for ten minute sessions. I know several psychiatrists whose practice consists primarily of ten minute medicine sessions. It is not unusual for them to have three or four people in their waiting room, lining up for ten minutes of time. Obviously there is a strong financial inducement for psychiatrists to restrict most of their office time to prescribing medicine.

As a result of the two factors mentioned above, probably well over 50% of psychiatrists have abandoned their role as therapists and confine their practice to the prescribing of psychotropic medicines. Managed Care Organizations prefer to shift therapy to Ph.D. psychologists and to Master's level social workers, pastoral counselors, and other licensed therapists. In this arrangement the MCO's save money in paying for long term psychotherapy. At the same time they are willing to pay psychiatrists to prescribe medications with the expectation that medicines will reduce the morbidity of the individual and, thereby, decrease the need for therapy. In doing "medication management" psychiatrists generally see patients as infrequently as every 60 or 90 days or even less often. It is noteworthy that one nationwide MCO will not authorize or pay for psychotherapy by a psychiatrist, thus clearly relegating the physician's role to prescribing only.

This shift in psychiatrists' interest and practice has placed them more squarely in the field of scientific medicine. Here they are called upon to confront measurable symptoms, best standards of practice, and cost-benefit ratios. In brief interviews they can ask the simple questions which will provide them with some measures of improvement. "Are you feeling better or worse?" "Is your sleep better or worse?" "Do you still cry daily?" "How often do you cry?" "Are the voices still there?" "How often do you hear them?" "Do you still have thoughts of harming yourself?" "How often do you have them?" A ten minute interview is plenty. The pharmaceutical companies inundate psychiatrists with information about psychotropic medicines and give them copies of their "unbiased" studies about the efficacy and reliability of this or that drug. Keeping current with the psychopharmacological research is very time consuming but is increasingly necessary as this becomes an essential component of practice. In response to all of these factors, I suspect that many psychiatrists spend more time keeping up to date with psychotropic medicines than they spend getting current information from the patients they see.

In the mid 60's I was a member of the American Psychiatric Association's committee on Relations with Psychology. Most members of the committee were concerned that psychologists were making inroads into the domain of psychiatrists by setting themselves up as independent practitioners of therapy and by making "psychiatric" diagnoses. At some point, "turf wars" always involve money whether they are over land in the Middle East or over professional practice in the U.S. I had my doctorate in clinical psychology at the time, but since I was practicing psychiatry my bias was clearly with the latter. However, I took the position that psychology should chart its own course and supervise its own profession. We had some heated discussions but never reached any clear recommendations. And all the while, psychology marched on.

Currently the American Psychiatric Association is involved in a new war with the psychologists who are striving to bring about legislation which would allow psychologists to have limited prescribing privileges. When the battle waged over who could do therapy, there was room for comparisons in the area of training. Psychiatrists were frequently involved in the education and training of psychologists. They spoke the same language. They had many of the same professional ancestors. One could argue that one year of internship for psychologists was not equivalent to three years of psychiatric residency, but one could not say that the techniques or the theoretical underpinnings of therapy were different. Presently there are various other professionals at the doctoral and master's level who are doing therapy. The question is no longer, "Who can do therapy?" but "Who can do good therapy?" When it comes to the issue of prescribing privileges, one cannot make a reasonable comparison between the two professions that are at odds over this. Psychiatrists are first of all physicians. They completed medical school with all the training in sciences that involves. It is that background and that education that equips them to prescribe and is the basis of their license to do so. The training of psychologists is in no manner and in no measure comparable.

During my time spent in private practice since the advent of MCO's, I refused to confine my work to writing prescriptions for psychiatric patients. I had excellent training in psychotherapy and doing therapeutic work was one of the main reasons I was attracted to the field. In addition, I believe that persons who require psychotropic medications have more going on in their lives than just a chemical imbalance. I always judged that I needed to know more about them than just enough to decide whether or not medicine might be of help and which medicine might be the best choice. Even when a medicine was selected, I would not make the assumption that seeing the patient every month or two for 10 or 15 minutes was sufficient to give me the information I needed to determine whether or not the current medicine continued to be the correct medicine and in the correct dosage.

Too many psychiatric patients are given an early diagnosis and then medicated in keeping with that diagnosis and with little further psychiatric evaluation other than brief meetings every one to three months. The person may be getting therapy from a psychologist, social worker, or other professional, but in my experience there is little or no communication between the therapist and the prescribing doctor. I believe that diagnosis is an ongoing issue with persons who have emotional illnesses, and to be content with an initial diagnosis and continue to medicate accordingly can be a grave error.

Several years ago 29 year old Betty was referred to me by a former patient. She gave a history of mental health care since age 15 when her parents took her to a psychiatrist because she was despondent after breaking up with a boy friend. She was diagnosed with depression, and an antidepressant was prescribed for six months. She also saw a social worker for therapy for almost one year at that time. She had been in and out of therapy since age 15. "I would get bored with it and quit." At age 19 she had another episode with marked obsessive features, insomnia, and paranoid thinking. Betty returned to psychiatric care and was given different antidepressants. During the 10 years prior to our first visit she had seen four different psychiatrists and several different therapists with a variety of diagnoses including Bipolar Disorder, Major Depressive Disorder, Anxiety Disorder, Obsessive Compulsive Disorder (OCD), and Borderline Personality Disorder.

During our first interview she appeared extremely anxious, frightened, and rather desperate for some relief from her current inner turmoil. She focused on the diagnosis of Obsessive Compulsive Disorder which was made by the last psychiatrist she had seen. Symptoms which interfered with her life included counting things, checking things repeatedly, knocking on wood when anxious, and obsessive worrying. She feared that she was "going crazy" because of her inability to control these thoughts and behaviors. No one had explained OCD to her. She was reassured to know that people with OCD obsess about the worst things they can think of, and of course, going crazy is one of them. I told her that I never knew anyone who went crazy as a result of the symptoms she was describing. I also explained to her, as I usually do to OCD patients, that she had a "flypaper mind." We all have wild and ridiculous, insignificant and meaningless thoughts that come in and out of our heads in the course of a day. They are like flies flying in and out of a room when the screen door is open. But her mind has some flypaper in it, and when a wild thought gets her attention as it comes flitting through, it gets stuck on the flypaper. We all know what happens when we try to shake a fly off flypaper. The harder we shake the more it gets stuck. Patients are often reluctant to talk about their symptoms because they seem "so crazy." A 12 year old girl with OCD wanted me to watch the TV series "Monk," the OCD detective, so "you can see what it's like for me." She never wanted to tell me much about her obsessions or her rituals because she thought they were "too weird."

Betty's childhood seemed rather ordinary at least as provided in initial interviews. She had three younger siblings, two of whom had received outpatient therapy. Her parents did not get along well and finally separated when she was 16. She denied any history of physical or sexual abuse or any prior history of substance abuse. She was an average student through grade and high school. She did not participate in any sports or school activities. She described herself as being frightened of peers and always having a vague feeling of "something going wrong." Her anxieties were fed by her father's frequent lectures about how unsafe the world is and how untrustworthy people are. She attended college in the South and obtained a B.A. degree in health sciences. She said she was so depressed in college that she could hardly function. Her numerous fears and her OCD symptoms were rampant at that time.

I began therapy on a weekly schedule and during the first several months witnessed a wide variety of symptoms. She described "crying hysterically" for hours and had made threats to others about jumping off a balcony. On occasion she described paranoid thoughts about people watching her and following her with the intent to kill her. She would drift from one buying compulsion to another and complained about not being able to control them. There were clear periods of depression with statements of despair, wanting to sleep all day, and "wishing that a car would hit me." There were times when she slept poorly, increased her activities and her contacts with others, and had "irrational energy and an urge to do lots of things." She frequently talked about fearing that "something terrible is going to happen." During some office visits Betty appeared depressed and would cry throughout the entire session as she talked about things from her past. At other times she was euphoric and talked rapidly about things she was anticipating doing.

As I came to know her better and saw her pathology in action I was not surprised at the list of diagnoses Betty had received over the years. It was challenging to sort through the complex history of this young woman in an attempt to help her find a more stable and more comfortable life. Over the course of the first three months of treatment I came to recognize that she was a very intelligent and well informed person with a fine sense of humor and an acute sensitivity to others. All of this was present in spite of her multiple and, at times, overwhelming symptoms. She had researched most psychotropic medicines on the internet and had a better familiarity with some of them than I had. We frequently discussed possible diagnoses and possible medications. I gave her considerable latitude in deciding with me which drugs we might try, and over a period of two years we tested several different medicines. She was obviously gratified by this "team" arrangement and very cooperative in reporting possible benefits and side effects.

As we probed more deeply into her earlier years it became clear that she had never achieved any sense of value as a person and especially as a woman. Her mother was a poor example of femininity, and her father consistently showed contempt for all females. She never felt successful at school and was always uncomfortable with peers. She often said, "I don't bond well." She was uneasy in social situations and felt unable to carry on a coherent conversation. She always felt uncertain in any decisions she made, and she saw herself as "an easy mark for others." She expressed contempt for all men and was critical of women for being subservient to men. Her parents were her models for both of these opinions.

One day after about 18 months of therapy we were again discussing family issues relating to her childhood, and grade school was mentioned. She repeated what she had previously said about being "just an average student." However with some further probing, she added the information that as a child she had poor reading comprehension, poor math skills, and took hours to do her homework. "I couldn't pay attention to what I read. I would float off into space." The same thing would happen in class. She was always embarrassed when the teacher called on her because she could never pay close attention to what the teacher was saying. She said, "I would lose my notebook. During tests my mind would go blank. I'd phase out and doodle." In my office was a very bright young woman who never did well in school even though she put a great deal of time and effort into it, at least in earlier years. Could she have Attention Deficit Disorder? We pursued the discussion of symptoms. She mentioned "blurting out things" and then feeling awkward. She described low frustration tolerance, poor money management, procrastination, and being distracted even in intimate situations. She was willing to try the use of a stimulant medicine.

Not many things are dramatic in psychiatry, and we become accustomed to expecting change to be slow. During Betty's next visit two weeks later she described the change, "It is so nice. I am calm, but not docile. It lasts about six or seven hours after I take the medicine. I can be attentive now to sounds and to how my cloths feel on my body. I can read and comprehend. I can recognize when my mind is wandering." In later sessions she reported being less irritable with others and getting along better with family members and with friends, all of whom commented on changes they saw in her. She could now enjoy social interactions, and she was able to attend to what other people were saying. Paranoid thinking ceased. Mood became more stable with some evidence of continued depressive thinking. There was a strong genetic background for depression and OCD. Symptoms of the latter increased and were treated with one of the antidepressants which can be effective for Obsessive Compulsive Disorder. Anxiety markedly decreased. As long as I was seeing her she continued to comment about how much her life had changed with our discovery of her attention deficit.

Betty began to see herself in a more positive way and decided she was ready to consider dating. All of her prior involvements with men had been sexually degrading and emotionally demoralizing. She met a man in her work setting. After seeing one another for several months in what appeared to be a healthy and mutually respectful relationship, they were considering marriage when I left the area. I referred her to someone for follow-up care. At that time Betty was continuing on Luvox for her Depressive Disorder and her Obsessive Compulsive Disorder and on Adderall for her Attention Deficit Disorder. This case history was presented as an example of the need for continuing review of the accuracy of diagnoses. Betty had the attention disorder from childhood. No one had ever asked the right questions before, including myself.

I am convinced that psychiatric diagnoses are often made too quickly and with too little evidence. I believe this is especially true with teenagers. I have seen a number of adolescent patients both in the hospital and in my private practice who were, in my opinion, misdiagnosed with Bipolar Disorder, which is also known as Manic Depressive Disorder. Non-professionals refer to it as "mood swings," and it has become a popular comment. "He suffers from mood swings." "She has been diagnosed with mood swings." Everyone has fluctuations in their emotional level and responses especially young people. This is a very serious diagnosis for anyone when one considers the treatment that is recommended. If someone clearly has a Bipolar Disorder, the treating physician needs to consider whether or not this person should remain on a mood-stabilizing medicine indefinitely. The theory supporting the continuing use of medicine is based on evidence indicating that the more frequently a person with this illness has an episode the more severe and more frequent future episodes will be. The medicines typically used for this disorder are not without possible serious physical consequences.

Of the hundreds of teenagers I have treated over the past 50 years, I can say that there have not been more than ten to whom I would confidently give the diagnosis of Bipolar Disorder. I have seen a number of youths who were heavily involved in the abuse of alcohol and sundry other drugs and who were diagnosed with this illness before there was an adequate time for the drugs to clear their system. An accurate diagnosis is difficult if not impossible to make while a person is still experiencing the effects of alcohol or drug abuse. When one considers the criteria for making a diagnosis of bipolar disorder, it is not too surprising that teenagers get this label. Depression is not an unusual diagnosis in juveniles and ranges from minor to serious. It usually responds well to treatment; it may or may not be recurrent; and it may or may not require the use of antidepressant medicine. The diagnosis of Bipolar Disorder requires periods of depression and of mania.

I will mention each of the criteria for mania (from DSM-IV) and suggest how each might describe fairly normal adolescent behavior. One criterion is "inflated self-esteem." I have often seen teens who were quite boastful especially around peers but who, in fact, lacked self-confidence. Another criterion is "decreased need for sleep." I often wonder how modern teens get along on five or six hours of sleep, staying up late to talk in chat rooms or on their cell phones or playing Nintendo. Being "more talkative" is another criterion. When young people find something to get excited about, they can prattle on, and at other times they can be quite taciturn. "Racing thoughts" and "distractibility" are two other criteria of mania. Youth have much that is happening in their lives these days with cell phones, text messages, school, work, social life, laptops, iPods, and Game Boy. Their thoughts must be moving very rapidly at times to keep up with it all. Two additional criteria are an "increase in goal-directed activity (either socially, at work or school, or sexually)" and "excessive involvement in pleasurable activities that have a high potential for painful consequences (e.g., engaging in unrestrained buying sprees, sexual indiscretions, or foolish business investments)." Fluctuations in behavior are characteristic of adolescent development. They rush into something full speed and then quickly lose interest and enthusiasm until the next attraction comes along. Sexual indiscretions and substance abuse are not uncommon in modern adolescents and certainly can have painful consequences.

In the past decade there has been a marked increase in the frequency of this diagnosis for teenagers. I question whether it is driven by "medication management" with inadequate talking time to make an accurate diagnosis or if many psychiatrists have lost touch with the current complexities of the adolescent environment. I believe Bipolar Disorder is a very serious label to give a youngster, and one that has very significant treatment implications. On occasion a second opinion may be in order.

There may be another factor at work in some of the diagnoses used in hospitalizing patients. Insurance companies have generally refused to pay for psychiatric inpatient treatment of persons with substance abuse problems. Consequently for someone who is abusing drugs or alcohol to be admitted to a psychiatric hospital rather than a rehabilitation facility, that person must have a psychiatric diagnosis. I might add that it is difficult to get approval to admit anyone into a psychiatric hospital unless there is a substantial threat of serious harm to oneself or to another person. The MCO reviewer, who of course never sees the patient, must be convinced of some danger before authorizing payment for the admission.

After admission to a psychiatric hospital, the treating physician must then justify continued stay to the insurance reviewer, and this requires a significant diagnosis. Depression is a good diagnosis to work with because it carries a potential for self-harm. Bipolar Disorder is even better because it includes the possibility of self-harm plus an element of impulsiveness and unpredictability. Diagnoses in psychiatry are not as rigid or as well defined as in physical medicine. The psychiatrist has considerable leeway in finding adequate symptoms on which to base a sufficiently serious diagnosis to gain a person's admission to the hospital and then to maintain the patient there for at least a few days. Unfortunately the name of the illness is to some extent driven by MCO limitations on providing suitable treatment.

The emergency room doctor cannot simply say to the insurance company reviewer, "Johnny is having a lot of difficulty coping with the death of his best friend in a car accident when Johnny was driving. He is feeling guilty, ashamed, and very sad. I think he should be in the hospital for a few days so that we can observe him, be sure he's safe, and then look to whatever further care is appropriate." Instead the physician is likely to say, "I have a 16 year old male who is seriously depressed after being the driver in an accident which caused the death of his friend. He is tearful and reticent to respond in the interview. He is unable to contract for safety. Because of a potential for suicide, I recommend hospitalization so we can treat his depression aggressively with antidepressant medication."

There is no clear evidence at this point that Johnny has a clinical depression, is suicidal, or should be started on an antidepressant. But MCO's do not allow for the luxury of two or three days in a psychiatric hospital just to provide further evaluation in a safe setting. Instead, a major diagnosis must be made and treatment must begin. When I was a resident in psychiatry many years ago, we were taught that when a patient came into the hospital we should take several days of observation before we began to solidify our diagnosis and decide on a plan of treatment. Now the insurance company wants a medication regimen and a treatment plan on admission.

I would like to comment further on a diagnosis I mentioned in Chapter I. In the prior reference I was writing about people who seemed to be "overly emotional" and suggested that they are often labeled as Borderline Personality Disorders. Certainly we do meet such people in the psychiatric profession. Some of their symptoms include unstable relationships, an uncertain sense of self, impulsivity, inappropriate anger, and feelings of emptiness. My quarrel is not with the validity of the diagnosis but with the frequency of its use. It seems to be used more frequently with inpatients and with those who are seen in outpatient clinics where multiple staff are involved in treatment. Patients who complain a bit too much, who object to some of the rules, who have difficulty relating to staff, and who respond emotionally to others often seem to get the "Borderline" label. Once the term is used, one can note a distinct change of attitude in many staff toward that particular patient. One hears treatment personnel refer to "The Borderline," and everyone assumes a rather guarded response in any exchanges. If one considers the symptoms mentioned above, such an attitude among treatment personnel seems far from therapeutic. When I worked with other staff in clinics or hospital settings, I let them know that I was opposed to Borderline Personality Disorder as a working diagnosis until all other diagnostic possibilities were carefully reviewed. I found the diagnosis was used too often for patients who were difficult to work with, who created management problems for staff, or whom staff could not fit into neat diagnostic packages.

Emotional illnesses do not coalesce into tidy bundles that are easily tagged with a name. Humans are very complex creatures, and emotions have a propensity to spread and contaminate a larger area over time. By contrast, physical ailments are more typically located in a discrete organ or system of the body. However, it may require a number of tests to determine just where physical pathology is localized. My wife recently had an episode of diffuse pain and tenderness in the abdomen. Extensive tests were done to determine the cause. They included a number of blood tests, an X-ray, an ultrasound, two CT scans of the abdomen, an endoscopy, a MRI, and a hydascan. The end result was surgery to remove a diseased gall bladder.

Mental illness is never so well localized and will never be so easily eliminated. Among the criteria for most psychiatric diagnoses, there is usually the following statement: "The disturbance causes clinically significant distress or impairment in social, occupational, or other important areas of functioning." It is this distress that brings a person for treatment just as tenderness in the abdomen, severe pain in the chest, or another physical symptom brings a person for medical care. The next step is to determine what is causing the distress or the pain and to decide what can be done to relieve it. The only tests psychiatrists have are their own observations and those of others and information gathered through doctor-patient verbal exchange. When we consider the list of tests my wife had over the course of six days, tests which literally see inside organs and cavities of the body, it is obvious that it takes time to accurately diagnose psychiatric illness. One of the most important reasons for hospitalizing a psychiatric patient is that it provides markedly increased observation time as well as opportunity for verbal exchange.

Psychiatric treatment comes about in a number of different ways. Usually an individual realizes that there has been a change in mood, in thinking, or in behavior that has created or seems likely to create difficulties in life, and the person decides to find out if talking to someone might help. When people are overwhelmed by events in their lives or when their emotions seem overpowering, it seems natural to want to "talk to someone." While waiting for a bus, traveling on a plane, standing in line at the store, or waiting on a street corner, we have all had the experience of having a stranger begin telling us his or her life story. Some people seem to need to "talk about it" when things are not going well. Their approach to psychiatric care and therapy is a positive and cooperative one.

There are others who come to psychiatrists and "don't want to talk about it." They may have come of their own choice but feel awkward in talking about themselves to a "stranger." They may be there because a spouse, an employer, a judge, or a parent noted "significant distress or impairment" and gave them an ultimatum, "Get help or else." The reluctant patient is typically rather difficult to work with at least in the beginning. Teenagers are by nature usually uncommunicative initially and, more often then not, will say they don't want to be there. I have had adolescents in treatment who told me that they saw a previous therapist for months and never said much of anything. If after two or three sessions a teen continues to be unwilling to open up and discuss some meaningful issues and if there is an expressed desire not to come back, I bring the parent in with the youngster and tell them both that I do not see any benefit in continuing the sessions at this time and under these circumstances. I believe that therapists should not continue to see unwilling and uncommunicative teenagers for weeks and months in unproductive sessions.

It is sometimes difficult to determine whether or not treatment is indicated and for whom. One must bear in mind that treatment injustices can and do occur. Parents bring teenagers for treatment and provide information that may or may not justify care. The information provided by the parents is assumed to be correct and honest although the youngster may deny that much of it is true. This presents no dilemma for many therapists because the majority of parents report accurately on the behavior of their children. However, parents may be exhausted from conflicts at home and be searching for some relief wherever they can find it. When I was the director of an adolescent inpatient program, I recall seeing a number of patients admitted from emergency rooms based on reports given by parents. On occasion the youngster had denied the charges throughout the admission process but to no avail. It later became clear that the parents' statements had been grossly exaggerated. I remember a 15 year old girl who was admitted on the basis of her mother's claim that she was aggressive toward her and had been destructive of school property. We later learned that the destruction of school property consisted of participating in a food fight in the cafeteria, and the aggression toward her mother was verbal only. She was discharged 36 hours after admission because there was no basis for keeping her in the hospital.

Emergency room physicians are sometimes caught in a situation that poses a difficult decision. Should the doctor believe the calm, logical, composed husband who says that his wife has been threatening suicide for days and a few hours ago took a kitchen knife and tried to cut her wrist, but he restrained her and brought her to the emergency room? Or should the doctor believe the tearful, disheveled, distraught woman who states that she just discovered her husband has been having an affair, and when she confronted him he became verbally abusive? The woman does not deny that she made a comment about killing herself but says she did not mean it and has no thoughts of suicide. The doctor needs to think about the woman's safety and also about his own liability. Sending her to a psychiatric hospital seems to be the best decision.

Now the woman is additionally traumatized and can easily begin to think that her husband is doing this so that he can claim that she is an unfit mother for their two young children. (Such things do occur.) You can probably not imagine what happens at the psychiatric hospital. She is worried (anxious), angry (dysphoric), unhappy (depressed), suspicious of her husband (paranoid), eating poorly (possibly anorexic), refusing to talk with staff (uncooperative). It is likely she will be taking some psychiatric medicines within the first 24 hours after her admission. The insurance company will call the day of admission or the next day and will need a diagnosis and a treatment plan. If the report uses the words that are in the parentheses above and if medicine has been started, another two or three days of hospital stay will probably be authorized by the MCO. Doctors practice medicine somewhat defensively, and in this theoretical case, they might see it as safer for everyone to keep the patient another two or three days "just to sort through what happened."

When I was on the staff of a well known psychiatric hospital, the physicians responded to after-hour admissions on a rotation basis. After evaluation by a doctor in the emergency room of a local hospital, individuals were sometimes sent to our hospital for voluntary admission. The insurance company would approve the admission while the patient was in the emergency room. When the patient arrived at our hospital, the on-call physician was called for routine admission orders which were given over the telephone. Our medical director wanted the on-call physicians to prescribe psychotropic medicines over the telephone for each new admission. Most of us refused to comply on the basis that it was improper, if not unethical, to prescribe for a patient whom we had not seen. The director regularly ordered medicine over the telephone when he was taking calls, prescribing one or two of his favorite psychotropic drugs. I am sure his quick treatment response pleased the insurance companies.

When I had a practice in the West, I encountered the most reluctant patient I ever treated. Judy was brought to see me by her husband. An internist had referred her to me with the information that she had been arrested for theft and was facing a possible sentence with some jail time. Judy was a Native American of the Spokan tribe. She was tall, erect, with long black hair, and the strong, prominent features of her people. She appeared frightened as she entered the office, and my verbal attempts to make her more comfortable seemed to have no effect. Her occasional responses were in a low, deep voice and hardly audible. The hour proved tedious as I tried to put her at ease and, at the same time, gather a modicum of information. I explained slowly and quietly that her doctor had asked me to see her and that I understood she was charged with theft. I told her that after I spoke with her I would be able to write a letter to the judge and perhaps tell him something about what had happened and why it happened.

With a great deal of hesitation, long pauses, and halting words, she explained. She had a small restaurant in a nearby village. She had no employees and served breakfast and lunch to local customers. As she prepared lunch one day she realized she did not have a particular spice she needed for her soup. She closed the shop and left a sign on the door indicating that she would be back in one hour. She rushed to the large grocery store in the neighboring town. She shopped there regularly, but the store was so large that she was not known personally to the manager. She found the spice and then discovered that there were long lines at the two cash registers. She had to get back to start preparing the lunch which most workmen in the area would be coming to eat. She walked out with the intention of paying for the spice the next time she came to the store.

I firmly believed that this woman would not have survived being in jail, perhaps not physically and, for certain, not emotionally. It would have been worse than caging a wild animal. Not that Judy was in any way wild, but her spirit would not have tolerated the indignity. People use the expression "free spirit" to describe someone who thinks or lives a little differently. Judy had the free spirit of the Native American woman that she was, and although she accommodated well to our society, she never seemed to be of it. With my letter in hand, the judge dismissed the case and Judy got a "warning."

This became the strangest therapeutic relationship I have ever had. It was, in many ways, mysterious, uncanny, ethereal. Judy continued to see me for about three years at intervals determined by her, which varied from every week to once a month or even farther apart. We never made a "next appointment." She would call my answering service but would hang up when they responded. The answering service could only tell me that someone had called at a certain time from Judy's exchange area. I always knew to call Judy at the restaurant, and we would make an appointment. I never asked her why she did not leave a message. It was her way, and I respected it. At the time of her first appointment, my fee was $40. She paid in cash. After the fee was established, money was never mentioned again. She always left cash in an envelope on the table as she went out. During the period of her treatment my fees increased rather rapidly and reached $80 while she was still my patient. I never mentioned the change. She gave me a limited edition, Swiss music box for Christmas on three occasions. Treatment professionals are advised not to take gifts from patients, and it does raise ethical issues. Our connection was too sacred to be violated by the insult Judy would have experienced had I refused her gifts.

When Judy was 12 she witnessed the death of her mother and her eight year old brother. The three of them were walking along a state highway, and the two were hit by a passing motorist who never stopped. After that, Judy was raised by her grandfather, a stoic and rather punitive man. She married at age 21. Her husband went to Korea as a soldier and later returned but not to her. She married her current husband, Ralph, when she was in her early 40's. I always assumed it was a loving but not intimate relationship. She had a daughter from her earlier marriage. They had been out of touch for years due in part to the grandfather's interference. I encouraged her to reestablish contact with her daughter which she did. She enjoyed her two grandchildren.

At age 18, as a high school graduate, Judy began working as a waitress in one of the town's many good restaurants. She learned the business by observing, and she saved enough money to open her own small place in a village about 15 miles away. Her business prospered. Over the years, she purchased three houses and one church in the village. She refurbished and rented them. She was financially generous to the small community. She had three special charities. She encouraged some of the local poor to come by at noon each day and "sample the soup to let me know if it needs anything," free of charge of course. She did the same for local school children only with ice cream in the afternoon. Her third kindness was to stray dogs. Ralph built her a kennel to house them because she brought home every stray she found. She loved books and music as well as derelicts, children, and lost animals. Her husband added a small room to the house for her library.

She often brought a large book of travel or art and left it for me on the table with her payment. On one occasion she left a lovely, leather bound, blank-page book with gilt edging and trim. I still have the note which she left inside. It reads, "Always I had planned to fill this book with poetry and music, then hide it carefully away with the saxophone for someone to find years from now and wonder. It isn't going to happen. Your decorator made this room as lovely as a symphony so she can probably fill it with music with no effort. Someone should write in it. Books should not be wasted." Although we had never spoken of it, Judy must have known that my decorator was my wife. She learned on her own to play the violin, the piano, and the saxophone. She was elated when she found an old juke box and bought it for the restaurant. One day she told me her secret. Sometimes in the evening she would tell Ralph that she had something to do at the restaurant, and she would drive the four miles into the village. She would lock the door, pull down the shades, and get out the saxophone she had hidden there. Then she would play her sax, accompanying the music on the juke box. It must have been a wild but heavenly scene.

When I decided to move back east, I told Judy two months before I was to leave. It was a difficult moment. It was as if she tried to scream, but it never left her throat. She sobbed and rushed out the door. She was gone. The next move had to be mine. I waited about two weeks and then called one afternoon when I knew she would be in the restaurant. Her responses were brief, not angry but sad, not cold but flat. I told her that I really would like to have her return for another visit and that I thought we should talk at least one more time. She said she would call in a week or two. About two weeks later I had the call to the answering service with the hang up. I called the restaurant, and Judy made an appointment for the following week.

I believe the visit brought some sort of closure for both of us. I reviewed our work together and gave Judy some information about our moving east and spoke of the reasons for the change. I also gave her my new address and told her I would like to hear from her if she would care to write. Both of us knew that would never happen. On a small table in the corner of my office there was an old fashioned table lamp with a delicately painted half-globe glass top and hanging crystals. Judy had at times mentioned the lamp as a beacon in her life and something she would picture in her mind when she felt disturbed or worried. I told Judy that I wanted her to have the lamp. She was surprised and pleased. For a moment she raised some doubt that she should accept it, but then she agreed gratefully and gracefully. I had brought a box to the office large enough for the lamp. She left with it that day, the last day I ever saw her.

That is not the end of the story. About ten months later I received a letter from Judy's husband. Judy went out one evening after dinner to feed the dogs. When she did not return, Ralph stepped out to look for her. She had dropped dead by the kennel. In his letter Ralph said there was a lamp in Judy's library that seemed very special to her and which seemed to have some connection to me. "Would I like to have it?" I wrote a letter of condolence and also said that I would like very much to have the lamp. He sent it within a few days. It was in a rather flimsy box and was shattered. I thought I should let him know and did so. He later wrote telling me that he had taken it to someone to pack and send. He enclosed the insurance check they gave him. My wife and I bought a pair of candle holders set on branches with small birds. Judy lives on in many ways and in many hearts. I believe that anyone who has done extensive counseling has on occasion had a dim awareness of a dimension they do not comprehend.

A clinical minded person might ask me, "What was Judy's diagnosis?" My response would be, "I don't know." How could I know what her diagnosis was when I hardly knew who she was. I might say she was a Native American managing to cope in the white man's world. I might say she was a modern Saint Francis trying to teach us something about animals. I might say she was a self-made entrepreneur. I might say she was a maker of music and a lover of the arts. I might say she was a spirit that touched the hearts of many over a bowel of soup, a hot lunch, an afternoon ice cream, or a Swiss music box.

CHAPTER VII
Thoughts About Therapy

In our present society, therapy for emotional disorders comes in many different forms and is provided by a wide variety of individuals. The range of therapeutic methods includes approaches as diversified as aromatherapy, yoga, crystal therapy, craniosacral therapy and a host of other alternative medicine treatments which would not be included under the term psychotherapy. This chapter will be confined to a discussion of psychotherapy, some of its unusual aspects and limitations, and comments about various professionals who practice psychotherapy.

The usual list of psychotherapists includes psychiatrists (MD), psychologists (PhD, PsyD, MS, and MA), social workers (LCSW-C), and licensed clinical professional counselors (LCPC). Pastoral counselors are usually found in the LCPC group. The latter two professional groups usually possess a master's degree in their field. It is remarkable that many educated persons including lawyers, clergy, and business executives do not know the difference between psychiatrists and psychologists. After graduating from college psychiatrists complete four years of medical school followed by four years of psychiatric residency. After graduating from college psychologists typically complete four years of graduate school with unspecified additional training if they have their doctorate. If they have a master's degree, they customarily spend two years in graduate education. Psychiatrists are the only group who possess education and training in the entire field of medicine and thus have the background to recognize and distinguish physical problems as part of or separate from emotional illness.

The therapeutic expertise of these various professionals depends on a number of things and includes their education, their specialized training, and the amount of experience they have had. Over the years I have had the opportunity to teach and to supervise students in psychology, social work, and pastoral counseling. Sometimes I have had the thought that good counselors are born, not made. I'm sure that is an exaggeration. But I am convinced that some of the most valuable traits of counselors do not come from education or training or supervision but come from genetic make-up, innate temperament, family background, and one's own life experiences. We can teach empathic responses, but we cannot teach empathy. We can describe what it means to be non-judgmental, but we cannot stop people from making judgments about others. We can help trainees recognize emotional responses in others but not always in themselves. We can impart an idea of the importance of sensitivity, but we cannot impart sensitivity. We can teach them the techniques of therapy, but we cannot be certain they master the art.

Choosing a therapist is not an easy thing to do. First of all, it is difficult for a person to meet with a professional and accept the idea of telling this stranger some very private and personal things about one's life. Most emotionally troubled individuals have already developed some concerns about trusting others. After one or two interviews it is challenging for a potential patient to decide whether or not this therapist seems to be trustworthy, competent, and compatible. If someone sees a surgeon or a dermatologist about something and is not satisfied with the recommendation or the treatment, it is relatively simple to get a second opinion or to choose another specialist. The personality, the congeniality, or the sensitivity of the physician may be less than expected, but none of these is critical to the treatment process or the outcome. To obtain a fair assessment of a therapy relationship one must reveal a good deal about oneself and, at the same time, make some assessment about whether or not this therapist is a good match. A second or third visit may be necessary to feel comfortable with the choice. But while this selection process is going on, the patient continues to expose intimate life details which create an investment in the relationship. As a result, it becomes increasingly difficult to decide to look for another therapist. I have had patients who continued to see a prior therapist for weeks and sometimes months even though they did not feel comfortable with their choice. Their negative reactions varied. "He talked about his own life more than about mine." "She was always 15 to 20 minutes late for appointments." "He kept telling me that I should stop dwelling on certain thoughts." "She insisted that I should be taking medicine." "I didn't like her attitude." "He kept telling me that he knew just how I felt, and I'm sure he didn't."

It must seem antiquated to mention a person's reticence to talk to a therapist, when many people watch television talk shows where guests describe intimate details of their lives probably more graphically than is heard in therapists' offices. I would not attempt to understand, much less explain, what motivates the emotional exhibitionism that takes place on television. I do believe that people yearn to tell others about some of the unusual things that happen in their lives. Sometimes we want an opportunity to explain or, at least, to complain when we feel we have suffered an injustice. But for the vast majority of people it is rare that anything rises to the level of wanting the world to know. It must be otherwise for talk show guests.

I would never encourage patients to continue seeing a therapist who makes them feel ill-at-ease. This does not mean that therapy is always an agreeable experience. There is a difference between talking about things that make one feel uneasy and talking to a person who makes one feel uncomfortable. After all, changing therapists is a weighty decision, especially after someone has invested several hours of time and shared private concerns with the current therapist. For some people one of the unfortunate results of such a dilemma is to quit individual therapy.

Ideally therapy is terminated when the patient and the therapist agree that the symptoms or the problems that brought the person in for help have been sufficiently resolved. Some persons who come for care have discrete issues or symptoms which are settled with short term therapy. Other patients have major emotional problems which may be related to earlier trauma, to developmental deficiencies, or to genetic predisposition and which require long term treatment. Some of these individuals become discouraged with their progress and discontinue prematurely only to return at a later time when symptoms or adjustment difficulties again interfere with function. If they leave and return to therapy several times, they can become disheartened and begin to think that there is neither help nor hope available to them. This kind of cycle and this conclusion often occur when the goal of the therapeutic process is unrealistic.

The caregiver can give the impression that the patient is expected to leave behind, to stop thinking about, to disconnect from the trauma of the past. The message given is that symptoms will go away and emotional stability will return when the patient is able to comply with these expectations. Why is it that mental health professionals expect others to "get over," "to stop playing tapes from" the horrible events of the past, but they encourage them to enshrine and cherish the good memories of past and recent times. Memory is not like a computer that we can turn on and off. We control some memory functions, but there are some "on" switches that can be tripped by everyday events such as a phone ringing, a news headline, a tone of voice, a shadow on the wall, a loud noise, an odor in the air. And in response memory takes the person to some far off time and place which may be filled with dark fear, deep loneliness, crushing sadness, and overwhelming self-doubt.

Much of the trauma of the past is never forgotten. Some of it needs to be remembered more clearly, particularly when it was more subtle, so that the cobwebs of half-truths surrounding it can be dispersed. Adults often see their childhood in a neutral or even a good light when, in fact, it was a time of severe emotional deprivation if not manifest abuse. I have come to believe that obvious abuse in childhood may be easier to remedy than undetected ill-treatment in an apparently normal setting. Abuse that can be named, that cries out for relief evokes a response in the victim as well as in observers. It incites fear, anger, and rebellion. Abuse that is insidious can escape detection by the victim as well as by others, including the non-probing therapist.

Barbara had been in and out of therapy on four or five occasions by the time she was 62. Anxiety and depression were the usual presenting symptoms. They fluctuated in intensity but were never incapacitating. They interfered at times with social relationships and marital harmony, but more importantly they intensified her underlying self-deprecation and disturbed the harmony of her life. Each time she sought treatment she had high expectations of success. She was an intelligent woman, able to express herself well, and willing to discuss things quite openly. But therapy never seemed to bring lasting results. She was always left with the feeling that she had failed again because there were still times of marked anxiety that "came from nowhere," episodes of anger that were unprovoked and later recognized as unreasonable, and times of brief but isolating depression when suicidal thoughts emerged. Each of these negative events was interpreted by her as a failure on her part and evidence of something in her that was very evil or very disordered. When separated from these "failure times," she was a vibrant, energetic woman with a number of interests, a wide range of friends, and a keen sense of humor.

Barbara's history, on the face of it, was not remarkable or highly unusual. She was an only child whose father left when she was age 3. She lived with her mother, Kate, and her maternal grandparents. Her grandmother was her primary caretaker and undoubtedly overprotective. A maternal uncle visited frequently and made it his game to tease her in front of the others. No one ever came to her rescue. Her grandfather was probably her only ally, but he was not a strong figure in the household. He had a steady job and except for some "payday drinking" contributed his check to family expenses along with Kate, who worked in a clothing store. Kate was an active alcoholic who was regularly involved with a wide variety of male companions.

The above history of growing up would hardly be noted as abusive. But there is the saying, "The devil is in the details." Prior therapists had never probed into the details. At every opportunity Kate remarked about never wanting to have a child. She often said to Barbara and to others that her unhappy life, poor health, obesity, arthritis, and dentures were all because she had had a child. Barbara grew up feeling that she was a mistake and, as children easily do, blamed herself for anything that went wrong. Kate made it clear to her daughter that her father walked out because he hated her for crying so much as a baby. She never saw her father again until she was in her 30's. He did leave gifts for her as a child, gifts which her mother let her see and then made her give away. On occasion her mother would buy her a doll, and about the time Barbara became attached to it Kate would decide that some poor child in the neighborhood needed it, and she would make Barbara give it to her.

No one paid any attention to Barbara's grades, homework, or activities. She was rarely allowed to play with neighborhood children. She had no friends to talk to or with whom to share things. Adults in the household never encouraged her and never showed any interest in her feelings. Her mother regularly attended a variety of civic meetings, invariably taking her daughter with her even at an early age. Barbara had the fantasy of someday seeing her father at one of these outings. She had no private space, no private time, and made no personal decisions. Her grandmother chose the clothes she wore and how her hair was done. Peers teased her about her clothes, her hair style, and her mild obesity. She could not remember ever being asked if there was some place she wanted to go, something she wanted to do, or someone she wanted to see. However, in everyone's judgment she was "a good little girl." Her grandfather died when she was 12. His memory was contaminated by her mother telling her that he was angry at Barbara when he died.

She remembered worrying about displeasing anyone and feeling guilty if someone seemed unhappy. She remembered feeling sad and lonely as she talked to her dolls. Although she was a fearful, anxious, unhappy child she did well in school and responded to teachers who showed some interest in her. Her mother remarried about the time Barbara entered high school. This union did not change Kate's alcoholism or "nights out" by herself. Shortly after the marriage her stepfather threw away Barbara's childhood clothes and keepsakes when she was out of the house. Apparently he did this during an angry episode with Kate. After completing high school Barbara went to college but lacked confidence in herself and enthusiasm for the work. After two years she left and married a man who showed her little respect and less love, who berated her verbally, and on frequent occasions threatened physical harm.

Barbara's childhood was psychologically abusive, but the ill-treatment was overlooked by others and not identified as such by her. As a result, she took the natural step to blame herself for anything that went wrong. It was always "her failure" because she could not name the failure of others. As with most abuse victims, the miracle was that she survived with an intact psyche that could still reach out to others with love and tenderness. When we look carefully into the background of patients, we can always come to some understanding of why they are ill. The real mystery is how they manage to preserve the stability and emotional health they have.

Social interaction with peers during her adolescent years could have provided Barbara with an opportunity to view other families and to discuss with peers their home life as well as her own. Comparisons would have been painful but enlightening for her and may have encouraged her to engage in some rebellious behaviors which might have given her a sense of freedom, self-determination, and self-worth. Unfortunately her first marriage only continued the degrading experience of the earlier years. Nevertheless, life sometimes presents us with "corrective experiences," that is, events or people or situations that seem to propel us into a change of heart or of mind with a consequent change in our lives. It is difficult to say what corrective experiences came to Barbara. One was certainly the fact that her father asked her to visit when he was dying. It was a sad but graced reunion. Soon after that visit she decided to leave her abusive husband. It was a turning point in her life. Did the visit to her father convince her that he had loved her through all those years of separation, that he had never left her, and that he had never been angry at her? Did the visit begin to cast a different light on her naive assessment of her mother? Did it tell her that she had a right to respect and love from others?

Did therapy ever cure her ills? Not as she would have liked because it could not give back to her all the opportunities she might have had in life if her childhood had fulfilled developmental needs. But therapy finally gave her an understanding of the indelible damage that had been done to her psyche. She learned that the misery that intruded into her life was a product of her childhood and not something she had created or ever wanted. The history would remain part of her but contained by her gentle caring for her second husband and her children, her warmth toward countless others, her faith in a God she had clung to through the years. Her new perspective would give her solace and strength when the episodes of anxiety, anger, or depression recur, as they will, but now they will not be seen as "failure times." She came to know that she had not failed in therapy, but that therapy has limited benefits. One of these is to help a person live productively and gratefully with a psyche that was scarred by others who could not love as they should have loved, others whom the patient may now view more realistically.

We marvel at the strength and determination of individuals who overcome some physical handicap or illness against great odds. If a person is in an accident which results in a disfiguring facial scar or a damaged limb, we admire that individual when she or he can achieve a healthy life adjustment and accommodate so well that the scar or the limitation is hardly noticed. Similarly, when adults have serious medical conditions such as a heart attack, a stroke, or cancer, it is vital that they reach deep inside themselves to find the inner resources to reduce the impact on their health and their life. They fight not just to get well but to overcome any negative consequences in their lives. We recognize that they do not get better just by thinking about it or just by willing it. In these situations we speak of courage, resilience, tenacity, perseverance. In other words, they bring the force of their emotions into play in order to achieve their goal.

This brings us to an important question. Since we know that those who triumph over a major illness or physical injury do so with the aid of their emotional energy, how do persons who have suffered severe psychological illness or injury recover when it is their emotional capacity that has been impaired or nearly destroyed? This is the real challenge faced by therapists, namely, to help people get well when the qualities they need to get well are the very attributes that have been damaged.

About 15 years ago I treated a 23 year old man who came to see me with the encouragement of his parents. Ben lived with them and his 14 year old brother. He had been receiving mental health care since age 15, recently by a psychiatrist who prescribed medicine and a social worker who provided therapy. His parents wanted him to make a change in caregivers, and he agreed. At the time I first saw him he was a recluse, seldom leaving the house and only doing so with a great deal of urging on the part of his parents. After completing high school he had gone away to college for one semester but was too depressed to return after the semester break. He slept poorly, had no social contacts, spent most of his time on the internet, and would become very apprehensive when either of his parents was out of the house. He described himself as feeling hopeless, not wanting to get out of bed, and seeing the future as dismal. Suicidal thoughts were frequent and, at times, quite prominent. He did not go out of the house because "Everyone is looking at me and laughing at me; they laugh at how I look."

He avoided looking in mirrors because he could not tolerate his appearance. This was all in spite of the fact that he was an average looking young man with no unusual or offensive facial or bodily features.

His previous psychiatrist had tried three or four different antidepressant medicines with no response. The lack of benefit is not surprising because Ben had never taken any of them for more than a few days. He never informed the psychiatrist that he was noncompliant with the medicines because "I was afraid he would get angry." After several weeks I did recommend an antidepressant, and I prescribed one with the agreement that he would tell me if he decided not to take it. After about two months he admitted that he thought it might be helping, but within another few weeks he elected to discontinue it. "I just don't like to take medicine," was his comment.

Ben had a very promising start in life. He was an excellent student, very popular with peers, admired by teachers, active in sports and drama. At age 15 he developed a complicated illness which necessitated several months in the hospital, three or four surgical procedures, frequent injections, and numerous blood tests. He remembered that he was angry and rebellious initially about all the procedures and at times fought with the doctors, the staff, and his parents over them. They kept telling him that it would be easier for him if he just accepted what had to be done. They finally convinced him, and he became calm, docile, and compliant with whatever they wanted to do. As he described the situation I felt I was witnessing something in him that was dying. He had in reality become passive, withdrawn, and depressed. Of course, medical personnel and his parents responded positively and praised him for the change.

After he recovered from the physical illness he left the hospital, but he left his spirit there. He returned to school but without enthusiasm for classes, for teachers, for peers, or for activities. He remained distant and became increasingly ill-at-ease with peers, who, in typical teenage behavior, left him behind very quickly. He described how difficult it was to be unable to find his way back to anything he knew before he became ill.

He was experiencing what many depressed persons experience, that is, loss of problem solving ability. That is a frequent but often unrecognized symptom of depression. Very depressed individuals have difficulty thinking; and the process is not only sluggish, it is also narrowed in scope. Thoughts focus on the negative, and imagination can only bring visions of a worsening world. Most people can recall waking in the middle of the night and becoming focused on some recent problem or on one they are facing. In the dark of night without any distracting stimuli the problem seems to take over the mind and fill it with doubt and images of disaster. The next morning in a brighter world with full faculties of mind and mood the expected outcome may appear less frightening and the solution may be obvious. Some people live in the night of depression, and after being there for months and sometimes years, they do not remember that life can be and should be brighter.

When he first came to my office, Ben had lived in the blackness and narrowness of depression for six or seven years. He seemed to be a good candidate for medication, but it was not acceptable to him. We worked slowly and carefully to rekindle his interest and his imagination, to reinstate a more realistic view of himself and of the world, and to reestablish some contacts beyond his current hermitage. He drove to the office for his weekly appointments. He began to expand his trips to include going to a mall in a different neighborhood. He always feared meeting someone whom he might know. He couldn't face answering the expected question, "What have you been doing since I last saw you?"

Most people engage in magical thinking of one kind or another. One of Ben's magical formulas was the following. When he walked in a mall he would look in the store windows and never at the people because "if I don't look at them, they can't see me." He continued to stretch his horizons, driving farther, eating a meal in a restaurant. He participated in internet chat rooms and met a girl who lived in another city. Eventually he traveled by air to visit her. The relationship continued and stretched his world. Before I left the area he had started college again and had chosen a field that seemed to fit his interests as well as his talents. In departing, I hoped that success in college, expanded contacts with other students, and a meaningful relationship with this young woman or perhaps another would continue to entice him out of the narrow recesses, the lonely pathways, and the bleak corners of his depression.

One of the positive signs I look for in patients is a sense of humor. It is promising when they are able to laugh, and it is predictive of a good outcome when they can laugh at themselves. As I think back to the patients I have mentioned in this book, I recall that except for one or two of them they could be amused in recalling some bad event of the past, laugh at some embarrassing mistake they made, or see the whimsy in a remembered solemn moment. In my experience the patients least responsive to the facetious side of things are those who are paranoid. Possibly it is the other way around, and it is the paranoid person who rarely finds reason for jest.

I was working with a charming schizophrenic woman many years ago. She had been in and out of the state hospital many times, and by the time she came to my office she seemed to be well stabilized on antipsychotic medicine. She made it very clear at the time of her first appointment that she was there to get a prescription for her medicine and had no interest in "any more head shrinking." I never learned much about her history, as a result. In any case, she was friendly and talkative and probably told me more than she intended. She lived out in the country with a male companion, possibly her husband. I never discovered the source of her livelihood. Among other things she collected unusual clothing and from her description she probably had clothes that would have dressed her for a role in any opera or play that was ever staged since the middle ages. She requested prescriptions that would last six months and would faithfully call about one month in advance for her semiannual visit. During one of these she began talking to me about some of her dreams. Because of my curiosity, which I like to think is purely professional, I thought this was an opportunity to "analyze" a bit. I asked, "What kind of dreams are you having?" Her response was immediate, "Why, schizophrenic dreams, of course!"

While working in a mental health clinic in the West, I set up a biweekly group therapy session for patients returning from the state hospital. They were an interesting and challenging group of eight or nine patients who developed a comfortable amity based mostly on their common experience of the hospital admission. One day they were talking about the bus trip that most of them had taken when being escorted to the hospital. On the way, there was a stop in another city with a two hour lay-over. The entire trip took about eight hours. One of the women was commenting on her journey and the unpleasantness of the time spent in the intervening city. She remarked very seriously, "The wait was terribly long and very nerve-racking. I thought I would go crazy." She waited a moment and then with a big smile added, "I guess I did." Her humor brought a laugh to the group and lightened everyone's load for a time.

Sometimes in doing therapy a humorous situation develops which cannot be shared with the patient. Years ago I was seeing a rather religious woman who was struggling with anxiety and depression. She called me at home one evening and said that she just had to call and tell me how much I had helped her in our session earlier that day. Since I could not recall any brilliant or even remarkable comment I had made during the interview, I had to ask what was so beneficial. She replied, "I felt so cared for when you took your rosary beads out to pray for me." She knew I was Catholic. She did not know that I consulted at the National Security Agency at the time and that the chain I removed from my coat pocket and put in my desk drawer during our meeting held the metal badge I needed to get into NSA each week. Patients like everyone else can find an unintended meaning in or a misinterpretation of something that is said or done. Therapists need to be alert to such possibilities in their work.

Patients occasionally ask me if there is any book that I can recommend for them to read. I have never recommended any of the self-help books partly because I have never had a patient tell me that a particular self-help book was of lasting value. There was a situation about 30 years ago when a middle aged man I was seeing expressed a keen interest in Thomistic philosophy. He had a good education with an extensive background in the sciences. But he had been captivated by something of Thomistic origin that he had read somewhere. Some years earlier when I was a student at the Catholic University of America, I had read the four volume work "Companion to the Summa" by Walter Farrell (Sheed & Ward 1942). It was a very readable book and an excellent introduction to the thinking of Thomas Aquinas. When I read books of that sort I frequently underline parts that are of special interest. I loaned what I thought was the most readable volume to my patient. When he returned it he was very appreciative especially "because you underlined all those passages you wanted me to pay special attention to."

There is an ever growing market for books that purport to teach people self-help skills. They are designed to give individuals some platitudes around which to regulate their comings and their goings, some sensitive sayings to guide them in relating to others, some proverb-like sentences to support them in times of crisis, or some sage truisms to bring them through current tribulations. The maxims and mottos are a bit more advanced but no more effective than the old adages, "An apple a day keeps the doctor away" or "Every day in every way I'm getting better and better." People are attracted to brief sayings that sound wise, noble, loving, generous, or virtuous. One can find them in a Benjamin Franklin maxim, a Biblical verse, a quote from the Dali Lama, on bumper stickers, and on the jackets of self-help books. How many of these have you ever made part of your life? "Practice random acts of kindness and senseless acts of beauty" say the stickers that show up in numerous places. I wonder what kindness and what beauty are born of them, and how many people have responded to them in any behavioral way. Why should values such as kindness and beauty be random or senseless anyway?

Self-help books have an authoritative "must read" style. The use of numbers provides an official, almost dogmatic tone, and the promises are of biblical proportions. Each book has its own number of hurdles to reach the "promised land:" 7 laws, 5 barriers, 10 ways, 13 lessons, 7 steps, 10 principles, 4 questions, 5 feelings, 36 hours, 10 rules, 30 things, 21 days. Since each book contains "all the answers to all these challenges," readers can prepare to receive the rewards when they complete the assignments. Prizes are specified in each book and include breath taking bounty: new friends, new business opportunities, new love, new confidence, a complete conversion of life, self-fulfillment, success in anything you do, total emotional and spiritual fulfillment, the life you always dreamed of, enlightenment, transformation, a sense of complete satisfaction with self and others, an improvement in every aspect of life, success and happiness, complete control over your life and your time, cessation of worry, confidence and power, and, last but certainly not least, an ability to control the behavior of others so that in an instant you can get anyone to do what you want, when you want, and the way you want and do it gladly. The last item is achieved by learning to use "conversational power." If these principles and techniques are so effective, one might ask why more therapists are not skilled in the knowledge, the expertise, and the power about which the self-help gurus speak.

The popularity of self-help books does prove that the majority of people share common problems. Most of us are concerned about our financial stability, our physical health, perhaps our body shape and size, the ease of our relationships with others, our propensity to worry or get angry or feel defeated. We want to have a sense that we are successful and worthwhile. We also share a common desire to have someone understand our problems. Self-help books purport to do just that. But that is exactly what they do not do. They may exhibit an understanding of "the problem" but not of "my problem." Each concern an individual has is unique to that person because that person is singular. One person's difficulty with anger, or with weight, or with relationships, or with finances is not the same as that of anyone else. If someone wants a vague general answer to a specific unique question, a self-help book has it. The author's "wisdom" may be based on some statistics, personal background, private convictions, religious affiliation, individual experience, or just plain entrepreneurship.

Therapists focus on the individual and on the special experiences and concerns of the individual. They do not give patients answers to their problems. They provide the opportunity, the freedom, and the time for those in distress to examine in depth the issues that trouble them. Caregivers believe that it is important for individuals to come to the point where they can with reasonable accuracy assess the situations which they need to confront and make decisions that are sound and healthy and within their capabilities. Therapists need to be aware of the limitations of their patients not in a critical manner but in a realistic and supportive manner. It is pure fantasy to believe that everyone can be anything they want to be. We all have a wide range of possibilities, but the extent of those is constrained by our genes, our life story, our beliefs, our desires, and our physical, mental, and emotional make-up.

Steve Salerno has provided a wealth of data regarding many of the gurus of the self-help movement in his excellent book "Sham" (New York: Crown, 2005). Self-help books give the definite impression that all you have to do is follow the formula as presented, and the goal of perfection, happiness, wealth, weight loss, sexual gratification, career advancement, personal prowess, marital bliss, or a body like Adonis or Aphrodite will be yours. They tell you that you are, in fact, entitled to whichever of those goals you desire. It is practically your birthright independent of any limitations of intelligence or other personal attribute, independent of any personal predicament you may have previously created in your life, independent of any previous adversity that may have befallen you, and independent of any limiting circumstances currently present. The only thing that can keep you from achieving your chosen goal is your failure to adhere to the formulas and rules set down for you in whatever "worth its weight in gold" book you are currently reading.

It seems safe to assume that most readers of self-help books do not possess a positive self-image. One can also assume that they begin their reading with the determination to incorporate the wisdom of the author into their own lives and acquire these promised changes. They are dedicated to adhering strictly and faithfully to the rules of engagement. They are looking for change, searching for help, striving for answers. They are ready to believe and to follow and to do what is recommended because they want to reach the "golden shore." They are like naïve religious converts who accept with blind faith rather than with intellectual appreciation and understanding the tenets of their newly found religion. They ride on the crest of a wave of exuberance and begin to tell you about this great book they are reading which, they insist, is already beginning to make a change in their attitude and in their life style. Months later you see them again. They look the same, act the same, talk the same. As they tell you about themselves, they mention nothing about any remarkable change, and there is no mention of "the book."

Mr. Salerno's book failed to emphasize strongly enough one of the ways in which self-help books can have negative results for their readers. One might say, "So they read a book, no harm done." Not so fast! How do they explain to themselves the fact that nothing really happened, that there was no improvement in their psyche, in their weight or in their shape, in their relationships, or in their pocketbook? Does this mean that they have failed again? The author convinced them before they bought the book that if they follow the 7 or 10 or 15 formulas they are guaranteed success. Readers rarely, if ever, doubt the "gospel" teaching of the author, especially if the author also has a successful TV talk show or has been featured on one.

They have one of two possible directions to go. They can believe that the failure is due to their own inadequacy and face the nagging fear that they will never change, never achieve their desired goal. Or they can assume the more palliative position that there was some change but not enough. In this case, the next step is to return to the bookstore for another book and perhaps another author who may be able to further their quest for transformation. No wonder the market for these books is booming. The more people read them, the more they think they need them. Supply increases the demand.

Liz was a 32 year old unmarried woman who was dedicated to self-help books when I began seeing her for therapy. During her teenage years she had been involved in a number of abusive relationships with male peers who demanded her compliance in substance abuse and sexual behaviors. Her father was demeaning toward her, and her mother offered little by way of positive modeling. She had avoided meaningful male contacts for several years. During therapy she decided to try to establish some positive interactions with men.

She became engrossed in several books which prescribed specifics relating to initial meetings and to extended association with males. The books became her source for decisions about a number of things. They told her when she could call a man, how much time should elapse between calls, how to respond during calls. They gave her guidance about what should be considered a date, how often she should see him, how long she should make him wait to see her again. Of course, there were many rules about intimacies, how soon, what, where, in what order, and then how to respond later in terms of calls and additional dates with essential information about timing. It was disconcerting to see this intelligent, attractive, capable young woman trying to find a recipe for successful dating instead of relying on her own emotional responses tempered by her own good judgment. She was gradually persuaded to do the latter, and she soon developed a rewarding and relaxed relationship with a young man.

Reassurance is defined as the action of removing someone's doubts and fears. This is precisely what is sought by those who read self-help books, those who seek therapy, and countless others who harbor the same feelings but somehow manage to contain them. What could be more reassuring than the claims on the jackets of these books? And what could be more deceitful and more disappointing? Therapists speak of reassuring patients, but the reassurance is based on a thorough familiarity with the patient's story, strengths, and potential. The technique must be used sparingly and must be based on the truth that surrounds this person and on a high likelihood of fruition. I warn students that trying to reassure a client before the student knows the capability of the person is very ill advised and weakens the therapeutic alliance. The relationship between the reader and the self-help books is more like an addiction than an alliance and, therefore, is not easily broken even with failed results.

Parents with problem adolescents are particularly vulnerable to those who market to their doubts and fears. Treatment of the wide range of emotional and behavioral difficulties of teenagers is very complex and involves a number of techniques and approaches. Whatever else is involved, I believe one of the essential ingredients in their treatment is the establishment of a relationship of trust and confidence with an adult who will listen non-judgmentally and respond thoughtfully and genuinely to whatever is said, an adult who is capable of hearing all that the youth has to say and in the process communicate respect, caring, and a sense of worth to the teen.

There is an excellent and informative book on the subject of the "troubled-teen industry." It is "Help at Any Cost" by Maia Szalavitz (Riverhead Books, New York, 2006). This book is important reading for any parent who is considering sending a teenager to a tough love program, a boot camp, or a wilderness program. Having a youngster in individual therapy two or three times each week together with family therapy and group therapy would not be as costly and would promise better results. Inpatient or residential treatment is sometimes an appropriate option. But whatever course is taken, the one-on-one relationship should be a required component. Szalavitz quotes research indicating that "no matter how sick or healthy a teen is, his insurance, not his symptoms, determines how much inpatient care he will get." A revealing comment!

In the beginning of this chapter we referred to therapists and mentioned the background of various professionals. Unfortunately we find gurus not only in books but also in "therapy" offices. Many of the "new age" Self-Help and Actualization Movement figures cross boundaries and set themselves up as therapists without using any title which would make them subject to examiners of training, credentials, or licensure. One of the most glaring examples of this transgression of boundaries is represented by the proliferation of "coaches." The name does not designate therapist. However, if they are involved with a client in a helping relationship that has the ingredients of serving as confidant, listening to emotional concerns or problems, exploring them more deeply, and trying to assist in bringing them to some resolution, it certainly sounds like therapy. These individuals come with a variety of backgrounds, education, and credentials. They are typically bright, quite verbal, and personable; and they sell their services to corporations and then to individuals within the purview of that connection. A doctorate in economics, philosophy, religion, or law does not qualify an individual to be a therapist. Does such a background qualify one to be a coach? That question cannot be answered because there are no stipulated qualifications for "being a coach."

If you decide to see Doctor So-and-So assuming that person to be a therapist, it might be important to ask, "Doctor of what and in what?" A doctor (Ph.D.) may be in psychology, counseling, or social work and, therefore, legitimately in the field of therapy; or the degree may be in anthropology, bacteriology, theology, oceanography or any of several other areas which, of course, does not qualify the individual to provide therapy. The reader is referred to Salerno's book for further comments about "coaches."

In discussing self-help books and credentialed therapists, it is important to note that there are many first rate therapists who have also written books that provide a wealth of information about emotional health based on their broad clinical experience and adherence to high professional standards. David Burns, Erik Erikson, Harriet Lerner, and Robert Coles are examples of these authors whose books are primarily informational and encourage readers to contemplate change without marking the specific route or promising Shangri-La.

Adam Phillips, author of "Going Sane: Maps of Happiness" (Harper Collins, N.Y. 2005), wrote a February 26, 2006 Op-Ed for The New York Times. One of his statements summarizes the principal point of this chapter. "Psychotherapy makes use of a traditional wisdom holding that the past matters and that, surprisingly, talking can make people feel better --- even if at first, for good reasons, they resist it. There is an appetite to talk and to be listened to, and an appetite to make time for doing those things."

CHAPTER VIII
Role of Religion

Much of this chapter will focus on the history of the interaction between formal religion and the field of psychiatry. We will also review some of the aspects of treatment faced by mental health professionals when they work with persons of various faith persuasions or spiritual dispositions.

In the first half of the 20th century several terms were used to refer to those who provided treatment for the mentally ill. Treatment terms included psychoanalysis, depth psychology, medical psychology, and psychiatry. Psychoanalysts, strictly speaking, referred to those who followed Freudian theories of mental constructs and treatment in their practice. The term, psychiatrist, has become an all inclusive term for physicians who are trained to treat these illnesses. There was a 50 or 60 year period early in the last century when there was a hostile relationship between organized religion and Freudian psychoanalysis. That is not surprising, since Freud considered religion an illusion and religious ritual a manifestation of obsessive compulsive neurosis. He was an avowed atheist who denied spirituality and freedom.

Spokespersons for various religious denominations took issue with these anti-religious views and in the process became highly critical of psychoanalysis. The most notable of these critics was Bishop Fulton J. Sheen who began radio broadcasts in the 1930's and in later years moved to television. He was a charismatic and popular orator who took up the task of attacking psychoanalysis and communism, both of which he considered anti-religious and atheistic. In his criticisms he was not careful to distinguish between the benefits of the therapeutic process and the philosophical underpinnings of psychoanalysis. Essentially he treated all "talk therapy" under the heading of analysis. His broadcasts were heard by millions of Catholics and others who were influenced by his persuasive powers and, as a result, came to believe naively that psychiatric care was a threat to their faith.

At this same time, psychiatry was a newcomer to the field of medicine and having some difficulty establishing its presence. However, when scientific medicine faced its helplessness to respond to the range of emotional disorders resulting from World War II, psychiatrists were available to provide care and in so doing gained full recognition for their discipline. Several of them who had served in the military were not only prominent in their professional field but were also leading members in their faith groups. A few of them took public issue with Fulton Sheen regarding his caustic denunciation of their profession, and one of them even took the matter to Pope Pius XII in Rome. In 1952 a number of leading Catholic psychiatrists formed the National Guild of Catholic Psychiatrists. The Guild did a great deal to educate clergy and laity regarding the field of psychiatry and the benefits of psychotherapy. In later years Bishop Sheen had a change in attitude and made the comment, "I can no longer speak of a great Catholic psychiatrist, but only of a great psychiatrist who is a Catholic."

In 1993 when I was president of the Guild, I proposed at our annual meeting that "Catholic psychiatry" was an aberration and that the Guild should be disbanded. All of us had been members of main stream psychiatry throughout our careers. Active membership had fallen from over 200 to about 12. The members agreed with little debate. Good psychiatry is psychiatry and not Jewish or Christian or atheistic. I believe the Guild had been formed primarily to combat the misunderstandings about psychiatry created by Fulton Sheen and those who supported him among the hierarchy and the laity. It also provided a forum for mental health professionals from various fields, religion professionals from various persuasions, and the general public to discuss ideas and issues which had emerged from this passionate controversy involving science, philosophy, religion, health, and social well-being. The Guild had been a successful response to those goals.

Other important events were occurring in the mid-20th century. The Catholic University of America opened a graduate Department of Psychology under the leadership of a priest-psychiatrist, Dom Thomas Verner Moore. The G.I. bill from World War II brought students from all over the United States to study psychology. Several prominent Catholic and non-Catholic psychiatrists served on the faculty. Publications bridging the span between therapy and faith issues multiplied. One person who contributed greatly to establishing harmonious relations between psychiatry and religion during those many years was Francis J. Braceland, who became the Administrator of the Institute of Living in Hartford, Connecticut. His book "Modern Psychiatry: A Handbook for Believers" (Doubleday & Company, Inc., New York, 1963) with co-author Michael Stock was one of his outstanding works. His name appears throughout the story of religion and psychiatry during the past century.

There was another significant program that must be mentioned in discussing the resolution of the antipathy that had developed between church and science as represented by psychoanalysis. In 1954 the Ham Foundation of St. Paul, Minnesota established a fund to support the Institute for Mental Health which conducted five-day summer workshops at St. John's University in Collegeville, Minnesota. Three such workshops were held each summer for almost 20 years. They were offered to clergy of all faiths as an opportunity to meet with psychiatrists and clinical psychologists to explore their common ground of caring for those who are emotionally disturbed. The premise for the programs was the belief that clergy are not only concerned with the spirituality of their flock but also with their human situation. By the time the Institute was discontinued in 1973 over 2,000 clergy had participated. I had the privilege of being a faculty member for nine years. It was an educationally stimulating, emotionally expanding, and spiritually deepening experience.

The above history is the story of institutions and organizations and positions taken by theorists and practitioners. These were battles over principles as they were understood and expounded by the ideologues and the innovators. While words were being preached, and argued, and written, and clarified, and discussed; thoughts were expanding, emotions were stirring, and points of view were changing. All this talk about and attention to emotions was catching on in the minds of students, teachers, theologians, clergy, and the public. People became aware of and interested in the novel concepts of the unconscious, unresolved guilt, the oedipal complex, neuroticism, resistance, oral and anal stages of development, inferiority complex, and other primarily psychoanalytic theories. Ideas gleaned from theories and practice made their way subtly but inexorably into the minds and the lives of the laity and church leaders.

Much of what I have referred to in preceding paragraphs has been associated with Catholicism. That is my background; nevertheless, it is not the reason for my focus. Theologians and clergy from many religious groups, both Protestant and Jewish, have been part of the struggle to clarify the philosophical foundations of various treatment approaches and their possible impact on the morals and faith of their church members. Edwin Friedman, an ordained rabbi and family therapist, comes to mind. His book, "Friedman's Fables" (Guilford Press, N.Y. 1990), is a delightful book I recommend to my students. There are many other writers who influenced this rapprochement between religious principles and mental health concepts. A few who come to mind are Harold Kushner, Billy Graham, Carl Rogers, and Henri Nouwen.

There are a few especially striking examples of the influence of "depth psychology" on moral issues and ecclesial principles in the Catholic religion. One might even suggest that the remarkable changes in the Catholic Church coming out of the Second Vatican Council (1962-1965) may have been influenced by the "mental health atmosphere" of the time. An awareness of the impact of the "driving forces of human nature" became obvious when Catholics who committed suicide were permitted to be buried from the church and in sacred ground. Prior to that change the presumption was that suicide was a grave sin of despair and could not be publicly condoned. That position was altered because the role of depression and its influence on the exercise of freedom was accepted. Soon after this change, the reality of emotional life and its significance in decision making entered into the area of marriage annulments. In previous times nullification of a Catholic marriage had for the most part depended on some definite impediment such as a prior valid marriage, concealment of a physical impediment to intercourse, or known sterility. The majority of annulments currently granted take into account the emotional condition of the couple at the time of the marriage and whether or not their emotional state sufficiently influenced their decision to have lessened the freedom required.

A third place where the Catholic Church has come to accept the principle that feelings can affect judgment is in dispensing priests from their vows. Patrick was a 35 year old priest who was referred by his bishop because he was discovered to have a romantic liaison with a woman in his parish. In therapy he acknowledged that a similar situation had occurred on several previous occasions. He was embarrassed and guilt ridden by his behavior because it violated his vow of chastity, but he felt powerless to control his desire for female companionship. His history was not an unusual one to find among clergy. His family was religious and quite conservative. His father was an attorney and was often absent from family events because of his busy law practice. His mother relied heavily on Patrick who was the youngest of three boys. He had always been a good student, active in sports, and popular with peers. He dated in high school and engaged in limited intimacy on occasion. In 12th grade he attended a special "day of prayer" given by the vocation director of the diocese. He began to think about becoming a priest, and when he mentioned it at home his mother was ecstatic.

He entered the seminary at age 18 and enjoyed his life there because it was "like a continuation of high school days except there were no girls." He had an inner loneliness which was persistent and disquieting, but his spiritual director advised him to "pray harder and God will fill the void." Six months before his ordination he was plagued by doubts about his vocation but was reassured by the same director that "this is a common time for cold feet." After several weeks of therapy he continued to chastise himself for his "perverse sexuality." Continued treatment helped him come to the conclusion that his sexuality was not perverse but thwarted. He decided to leave the priesthood. He was eventually dispensed from his vows and later married. I still get a Christmas card from him and his wife with pictures of their children. His dispensation was based on the constriction of free choice caused by emotional turmoil at the time of his ordination.

As we look at positive accommodations the Catholic Church has made because of a growing awareness of the impact of emotional life, we also find a dismal failure in relation to the scandal of child sexual abuse. It is not celibacy but emotional immaturity that is one of the primary causes of this behavior. In the past the seminary and the convent were eager to accept candidates at an immature age (before they were "contaminated by worldliness"). After entrance nothing was done to encourage their independent thinking or decision making. Unfortunately religious life does little to foster continuing maturation of the adolescent or the adult. Instead it expects continued dependence on the authority of others, and it provides a cared-for life. There are disgraceful examples of how those in authority have provided protection for sexual offenders who then continued the same behaviors.

Being a priest or a nun gives the individual a sense of worth bestowed by their calling and not something they have built from within and made their own. They see their value reflected back in the eyes of the faithful who were in the past too quick to forgive any transgressions. Some religious may have examined their conscience daily in the prescribed manner, but they failed to examine their life and their interactions with others. Immaturity and loneliness were a disastrous combination for a few and resulted in the ravage of youngsters and in their own disgrace. A number of churchmen in authority equally immature and isolated exercised their juvenile judgment and transferred offending clergy from place to place jeopardizing the innocence of children and the faith of believers. There is evidence that corrective modifications in age of entry, in seminary training, and in diocesan regulations are being made.

For several decades the question has been whether or not psychiatry and religion, mental health and spirituality, therapy and morality could fit under the same roof. Marked changes in attitude are occurring among some religious individuals and some church leaders. On August 31, 2006 the Washington Post published an article by Rob Stein titled, "Medical Practices Blend Health and Faith." The subheading was, "Doctors, Patients Distance Themselves From Care They Consider Immoral." The article stated that medical personnel are establishing practices and clinics where they can adhere to their beliefs and moral principles. They seem to focus on issues relating to contraceptive devices, abortion, sterilization, and in vitro fertilization. Some of the patients who were interviewed for the article spoke of no longer wanting to go to a doctor who "tries to talk me into something that I'm not morally comfortable with." These new clinics seem important for the spiritual comfort of the medical personnel who work there because they are not called upon to be involved in procedures to which they are morally opposed. On the other hand, I find it difficult to believe that a significant number of practicing physicians are not observant of the faith and moral stance of their patients and not willing to treat them in accord with their religious principles.

The attitudes addressed in the paragraph above have also begun to permeate the area of mental health care. This appears to be true especially among some Protestant Fundamentalist groups. Increasing numbers of those seeking therapy say they are looking for a "Christian counselor." They apparently believe that the one who counsels them should be of the same beliefs, presumably so the therapist can understand them better and be in touch with their needs.

I have treated atheists, agnostics, and believers including Catholics, Jews, Protestants of various denominations, Jehovah Witnesses, Mormons, and Muslims. I found it possible to elicit the information I needed from them to provide me with sufficient understanding of their beliefs and values. It is not a great deal different than getting data that will furnish knowledge about a patient's childhood and family background. It is not necessary for the therapist to know the parents of each patient, but it is important for the therapist to recognize their influence. It is not vital that the therapist understand the religious tenets of each patient, but it is valuable for the professional to appreciate their significance for this particular person. Expecting a therapist to be a member of one's faith group is about as reasonable as expecting the therapist to have lived a few years with one's family.

In the early days of the National Guild of Catholic Psychiatrists I knew some psychiatrists who joined the Guild in order to identify themselves as Catholics and thus attract referrals from church sources. It provided a business advantage. I have similar misgivings about those who market themselves as Christian counselors. The Accreditation Council for Graduate Medical Education has a directive requiring the incorporation of spirituality and religion in their curriculum. Sensitivity to these areas is an expected competency in psychiatric residency programs. "The American Psychiatric Association Committee on Religion and Psychiatry recommends that psychiatrists maintain empathic respect for patients' beliefs and not impose their beliefs on patients." The above quote is from the article, "Working with Spiritual Issues of Adults in Clinical Practice" by C. Yang, D. Lukoff, & F. Lu. in

Psychiatric Annals (SLACK, Inc., Thorofare, N.J., March 2006). They also comment that, "the clinician's primary goal is to promote patients' self-determination and not to be a 'missionary' for a particular value."

The suggestion that the therapist should promote the patient's "self-determination" could possibly be interpreted as a seduction by some religious sects which are suspicious of self-determination as opposed to adherence to church authority. If a Christian counselor will only accept ideas and behaviors that are deemed to be in line with the **counselor's** moral values, it suggests a breach of professional ethics. "Christian counselors" are as much an anomaly as "Catholic psychiatrists" are.

As we have noted, when psychoanalysis first came on the scene with new ideas about the treatment of the emotionally ill many church leaders were gravely concerned that this newcomer might pervert or at least confuse the thinking of the faithful and alter their allegiance. It is interesting that half a century later there are indications that the tenets and practices of certain faith groups may be blurring the boundaries of therapists and corrupting fundamental principles of therapy.

An unusual example of an amalgam of religion and psychiatry is present in the special psychiatric hospitals that treat religious men and women of the Catholic Church. There are three or four of these institutions in the United States and Canada. They represent a hybrid psychiatry, a return to the "Catholic psychiatrist" of Bishop Sheen. When treatment is church-organized, church-directed, or church-controlled, it cannot be considered disinterested, impartial, or independent. One can question the motivation for such specialized treatment. On the surface it suggests that Catholic religious have special needs, are special people, or require special kinds of treatment when they are psychiatrically ill. Mental illness continues to have a stigma attached to it. Being admitted to a psychiatric facility is somewhat traumatic. Do they go to a "special" facility to lessen the trauma of admission? Most Catholic religious prefer that others not see them as "special people." There are a few, however, who bask in the warmth of being "special." They are precisely the ones who would be far better off if they could be cared for with the rest of humanity. There is another more probable motive for this hybrid care for religious. Perhaps there is something they believe should not be exposed to public view. In the past decade everyone has become aware of the secrecy with which church officials have tried to cover the delinquent behaviors of their religious personnel whether it was alcoholism, theft, pedophilia, pornography-addiction, or adult sexual relations. What better place to hide for awhile than a psychiatric hospital?

Several years ago when I was on the staff of a reputable psychiatric hospital we opened a service for "religion professionals," as we chose to designate them. Priests, ministers, and nuns were admitted for treatment. They were housed among the other patients and attended therapy with them although there was some group therapy exclusively for "religious." We occasionally had difficulty with one or another who expected a privilege or a response based on his or her special status. These situations became good learning experiences for them. Their presence in the mixed population was never a problem. In fact, it was beneficial for them as well as for the lay patients. I was particularly impressed by a straightforward Methodist minister from the city who asked his parish to put a note in the Sunday bulletin telling the congregation where he was and that he was being treated for depression. I've also known religion professionals who informed their congregations that they had been away visiting relatives when, in fact, they had been admitted to a psychiatric institution.

The Catholic Church still does not trust mainstream psychiatry to care for its religious, especially when they need psychiatric hospitalization. They respond somewhat like the National Security Agency (NSA) or the Central Intelligence Agency (CIA) formerly responded when one of their personnel was suddenly admitted to a psychiatric facility. When I consulted at NSA in the 60's it was obvious that supervisors would become quite anxious about the psychiatric admission of an employee. Naturally they were afraid that the patient might talk about things that others should not know. Due to increased sophistication government agencies no longer react in such a paranoid fashion. However, based on their desire to keep things from the public, religious administrators continue to use church supported institutions. Professionals in these hospitals are undoubtedly competent and dedicated. The problem is that they are competent in their professional field but dedicated to the church. Consequently good care may be in jeopardy.

In these hospitals financial arrangements are quite different than in other psychiatric facilities. Insurance payments are not an issue because the religious order or the diocese pays the bill. Therefore, the physician in charge does not have to be concerned about those annoying Managed Care reviewers, and length of stay becomes the psychiatrist's prerogative. Stays of 12 to 18 months are common. One staff member told me of a patient who stayed for 30 months with a diagnosis of Borderline Personality Disorder. This topic was the focus of an article I wrote in Sisters Today, "Mother Church, Doctor Freud" (Sentinel Printing Co Inc., Saint Cloud, MN, September,1991). The article concluded, "A serious and penetrating review will be difficult, because as long as Doctor Freud wears a Roman collar the string attached to it is in the hand of Mother Church."

Many of the religious who are hospitalized in these places are in reality "involuntary patients." This is so because whether or not they want to enter the hospital they are told to go by their religious superior, and obedience to the word of the superior is an obligation in religious life. Once they are admitted they are caught in the bind of obedience again because they are not accepted back by the diocese or the religious order until the hospital staff states they are ready to return.

Father Gerard was a 59 year old priest from the Midwest who was sent to one of these Catholic treatment facilities by his bishop. The priest's local superior heard a report that the priest had been "affectionate" toward a ten year old child on the school playground. Father Gerard had a hobby of photography and took numerous pictures of children along with pictures of families. He also collected pictures of children from various sources. The latter included some photos of nude children playing on the beach. These were not photos he had taken, and they contained no suggestion of sexual posing or sexual behavior. Gerard's immediate superior became concerned about his "interest in young children," and after waiting several months he decided to speak to the bishop of the diocese about the matter. The two of them agreed that Gerard should go to one of the church sponsored hospitals for an evaluation. The obedient priest went as directed.

After a three day evaluation the hospital reported back to the bishop. The report included phrases such as "unusual attraction to elementary school girls," "excessive photographing of children," "secretive about his visits to the school," and "excessive collection of Disney-type movies." He was given a diagnosis of "Ephebophilia, non-exclusive (attracted to teenage females)" with an additional possible diagnosis of "Pedophilia (attraction to prepubescent females)." The summary noted "excessive amount of time he spends relating to children as opposed to adults," "excessive photograph taking of others, particularly young females," and "significant sexual addiction to pornography." None of these "charges" was substantiated by the history Gerard gave or by any reliable observation of others. "Excessive," "secretive," and "significant" were all the interpretative comments of a staff member whose competency could be questioned but whose dedication to the hospital and the church was evident. A period of inpatient treatment was recommended "sooner rather than later" because he was considered "at risk for future problematic behaviors."

Under obedience to his superior he reentered the same institution a few months later and remained there for over eight months. Documents relating to that eight month period of care referred to him as a "pedophile," and the summary letter from the Medical Director to the bishop stated that "He seems to have come to terms with his being a pedophile." He was now a "marked man" because that's what certain diagnoses can do. The contract he signed before his discharge included his agreement to return to a "Continuing Care Workshop" every six months for the first three years and then once a year for the subsequent two years. He was expected to attend individual and group counseling on a weekly basis. He was also to attend three sexual addicts meetings per week. The contract also included recommendations regarding rest, relaxation, recreation, vacation, and entertainment. Admonitions regarding diet, work, sleep, and exercise were included. He was advised to "get a massage once a week." Mother Church represented by the hospital was taking care of her own in an intrusive, arbitrary, and imperious manner.

One year after his discharge Gerard attended one of the continuing care workshops. The report sent to his superior mentioned repeatedly that he was having difficulty accepting the diagnosis of Pedophilia but recommended that continued therapy and his deep faith should help him in his acceptance. Two years later Gerard requested a second opinion regarding his diagnosis, consistently maintaining that it was not accurate. In response to his request religious superiors sent him to a different church related institution. That facility obtained the records from the prior one. After a few days of evaluation, they diagnosed "Pedophilia, nonexclusive type by history in remission." Diagnoses of Depression and Anxiety were also mentioned.

Sometime in the next year Gerard began seeing a different spiritual director who recommended a different counselor who referred him to a different psychiatrist. There was also a change of religious superiors during that same period of time. As a result of Gerard's urging, these four new professionals finally met together. Each had heard the same story from him, each had made an independent assessment, and each believed in his honesty. They all viewed him as an emotionally immature religious who had easily succumbed to those in authority. He accepted without question or argument his superior's original decision to send him to the hospital. He had difficulty accepting the diagnosis given by the inpatient staff, but he felt helpless to combat it since it came at him from all directions. He also came to realize that, unless he acquiesced to the judgment of the professionals and accepted their position, there was no end in sight for discharge. So he accepted their diagnosis in order to bring about his release. The situation sounds analogous to that of prisoners who are promised deliverance if they confess. From personality and from training Gerard was docile, pliable, passive, and complaisant. He was also alone, frightened, and trapped.

The four persons involved in his care discussed the matter at some length. They agreed that the reports received were unacceptable and were not based on fact but rather on the paranoia in the Catholic Church stemming from recent sex scandals. Minor incidents become monumental, threatening, and subject to gross exaggeration for those who are paranoid. Someone mentioned "Gerard and children" and suddenly the story grew and gathered mischief in comments about "unusual attraction," "secretive visits," "excessive photographing," and finally "collecting pornography." The four agreed that an objective assessment was necessary, and it should not be done under church auspices. It was agreed that the priest would be sent for an evaluation to the National Institute for the Study, Prevention and Treatment of Sexual Trauma under the directorship of Fred S. Berlin, M.D., Ph.D., at the Johns Hopkins University School of Medicine. This clinic has been designated as a National Resource Site by the United States Department of Justice. It is a highly qualified and respected facility with an excellent international reputation.

After all prior treatment documents had been obtained and evaluated by the Institute staff, a thorough assessment was completed. The report stated that Gerard had been "open and honest" and "not at all defensive" during the interviews. He was diagnosed with "Generalized Anxiety Disorder" and a "History of Depressive Disorder." His recent psychiatrist and counselor had previously stated that his only diagnoses were Depression and Anxiety. Among the conclusions of the report was the statement, "However, based on the evidence made available to us, there is nothing to suggest the patient, who has never in the past acted in a sexually improper manner with a child, would do so in the future." There was also a statement that he had never been involved in looking at or possessing child pornography.

The sad conclusion of the story is that the bishop was not influenced by Doctor Berlin's report. To this day Gerard remains unable to function fully as a priest. As far as the church is concerned, "Catholic" psychiatry is apparently more impressive, weightier, and more believable than psychiatry without the mantle of religion.

Religion professionals and mental health professionals are both interested in what people think, what they feel, what they do, and why they do what they do. Consequently both professions will always have a common ground and a common interest, namely, people and their well-being. Their basic "people skills" may be on a par, and their professional approach may often be the same. But their focus and their objectives differ from one another. It is there that they cross paths, and sometimes swords. The goal of the clergy is repentance, sanctification, and eternal life. The target of the psychiatrist is self-awareness, stability, and a fulfilling life. This does not mean that the religion professional is inattentive to the emotional world of the parishioner or that the therapist is unmindful of the hereafter of the patient. It might be helpful if we reviewed some of the ways in which clergy confront mental health concepts in their work and then look at how therapists encounter the tenets of religion and the domain of the spiritual.

Religion professionals (ministers, rabbis, priests, elders, mullahs) have become responsive to the political issues of the day and do not hesitate to enter the arena holding up their standards of morality. Some of them outspokenly condemn those politicians who do not agree with them and on occasion threaten religious sanctions. Leaders of various denominations are quick to apply the principles of a particular faith to a specific national controversy, and they often do it with considerable fanfare. They speak loudly about generalities and principles, but they rarely provide any convincing arguments for what they say. Instead, they rely on their "voice of authority" which is gradually becoming less persuasive for many people. Religion has become "a weak voice" in our society, and that may well be because it speaks "politics" and not "spirit," it appeals to "rectitude" rather than to "reason."

The voice of religion at the parish level has become increasingly dependent on mental health jargon and quick fix slogans as clergy face the complexities of their parishioners' lives. In his book "Harvard Diary" (Crossroad, N.Y., 1988) Robert Coles writes, "Especially sad and disedifying is the preoccupation of all too many clergy with the dubious blandishments of contemporary psychology and psychiatry." And later he adds, "Surely we are in danger of losing our religious faith when the chief satisfaction of our lives consists of an endless attribution of psychological nomenclature to all who happen to come our way." A few years ago I watched a T.V. show in which a man with a gun was threatening to shoot several others in the room. In response to the commotion a priest came rushing in, and his immediate comment to the gunman was, "Let me counsel you! Let me counsel you!" The show was not intended to be a comedy. It typifies the helplessness that must be felt by many clergy when they face those who come to them in the midst of heart wrenching loss, starkly tragic lives, seemingly insurmountable crises.

Much has been written about the question, "Does faith provide answers to human suffering?" And the answers are "Yes" and "No." Victor Frankl in "Man's Search for Meaning" (Washington Square Press, N.Y. 1963) writes, "Suffering ceases to be suffering in some way at the moment it finds a meaning, such as the meaning of a sacrifice." Faith can place suffering in a spiritual context that gives it purpose, but this assumes that faith can pierce the encasement of grief and pain that surrounds the sufferer. The lonely, isolated, desperate individual may find it hard to respond to the religion professional who talks about the God who loves and values every person. If "no one ever told me I was somebody," it is quite a stretch to touch or feel touched by a spirit. Our pastor's homilies often refer to the Passion of Jesus and the Resurrection as the road we all will travel at one time or another. In a quiet moment of contemplation one can appreciate the significance, the truth, the mystery of what he says. But when tragic events or fateful diagnoses shatter one's world and leave darkness and despair behind, the spirit withers and may find little nourishment in religious truths. The consolation of faith does not always penetrate the grief that surrounds the individual.

Therapists know that much of what they say to patients will probably not be immediately helpful. Mental health professionals are frequently reminded of their inability to take away the pain and suffering they see in their office every day. They know that time and talk will eventually bring some relief, and they accept the waiting. I often wonder if religion professionals do not become weary and discouraged with their own words and their own work when they find that their words of compassion or encouragement or correction or guidance seem ineffective. It seems profane to suggest that religion be thought of as a remedy in life, but it might also be valuable to consider it so at least for discussion.

Remedies need to be used in the right manner, at the right time, and for the right ailment. You don't take heart medicine for pneumonia. You don't apply a splint to a bruised arm. You don't have surgery unless you know it's necessary. One cannot expect religion to save every troubled marriage, to console every grieving spouse, to stabilize every drug addict, or to reduce all promiscuity. A religious faith and practice can be helpful in resolving difficulties in some marriages. Pastoral discussions with a couple may be remedial but may also indicate that additional remedies should be considered such as a marriage counselor, individual counseling, a 12-step program, or a psychiatric evaluation of one or the other party. And one must accept the premise that all marriages are not savable.

It is important to know what the ailment involves before assuming that religion is the suitable remedy. The same general comments could be made about the pastor's contact with the grieving spouse, the addict, or the sexually active individual.

One could write an entire chapter on "The Sexually Active Individual and the Religion Professional." Sex is a super-charged area in our culture. Product marketing is built on prurient interests. Many television series and movies focus on sexuality. Sexual behaviors have markedly changed in the past few decades, and sexual attitudes have been greatly modified. When we look closely at the situation, it seems that it is the sexual behaviors that continue to push the boundaries farther and farther, and the attitudes follow along behind as if to justify the behavior. Even the boundaries imposed by religion have experienced review and some adjustments. Positions regarding homosexuality, premarital sex, and contraception have been greatly modified in some denominations.

When religion professionals discuss sexual matters with someone they need to keep in mind the sexual climate in which the person is living. The pastor could, as was common in the past, simply lay down the rules with a "take it or leave" attitude. Some left and later came back; others never returned. Discussions about sexual issues are always a time for listening. In this area it is really important to know what the ailment is before trying to prescribe a remedy. And then it is important to know if this is the right remedy and if this is the time to apply it. Sexual behaviors may be related to loneliness, past trauma, body image, alcohol abuse, anger, or a number of other emotional or physical factors. "Concupiscence" does not explain sexual behavior; it only describes it. It is important to know and to understand what may be involved for this person. Religious beliefs regarding morality are based on the supposition that free will is present. In his book, "And the Sea Is Never Full" (Schocken Books, New York, 1999) Elie Wiesel writes, "Freedom is not a given; it is something one must constantly fight for. Freedom is not even given by God. Freedom belongs to the human domain. It is up to us to shape and nourish it." In the area of sexual behaviors it is not enough that persons know what is considered moral or immoral by their church, synagogue, or mosque. Those precepts need to be made understandable to congregants in a manner that their reason can accept, and then they need to "fight for" the freedom of which

Wiesel wrote and "to shape and nourish it" in order to bring their behavior into conformity.

The "Catechism of the Catholic Church" (Geoffrey Chapman, London, 1994) says the following about emotions, "Passions are said to be voluntary, 'either because they are commanded by the will or because the will does not place obstacles in their way." That is an unfortunate wording. Emotions (passions) are fundamentally involuntary, as we have seen in previous chapters. Only when they are controlled (commanded) by the will can they be said to be voluntary. Until that time comes, reviewing church teaching, admonishing, lecturing, and guilt enhancement will not be remedial but will only increase the individual's sense of loneliness and separation from God. Fortunately most homosexuals who have been treated in this manner have been able to maintain their faith through support from one another and also from outspoken clergy and laity.

In the book by Coles quoted earlier, he writes of being "tired of watching ministers or priests mouth psychiatric pieties, when 'hard praying' (as I used to hear it put in the rural South) is what the particular human being may want, and yes, urgently require." Churches are filled with "Hallmark homilies" on any Sunday of the year but especially on Mother's Day. Every year I wonder the same thing. Does the homilist really believe that all mothers achieve the level of earthly sanctity or heavenly reward that is attributed to them? Does the preacher have any idea that a large portion of the congregation may be sickened by the thoughts and feelings the sermon brings to mind? Mother's Day is difficult enough for daughters and sons of tyrannical, abusive, neglectful, or smothering women. Salt is a salutary Christian symbol not to be poured on old wounds. One could make similar comments about Father's Day sermons.

Some of my clerical friends have told me that seminarians are encouraged in their homiletics classes to tell stories about themselves and their families in homilies. That's about as relevant and appropriate as therapists talking about their personal lives to their patients. Those who come for therapy are there to talk about their problems with the expectation of getting help for them. Congregants are there to hear the word of God, to be moved in some graced way to become better people, to touch the "holy" and learn to appreciate the sanctity of the "unholy," to escape for a brief time their finite state, and to refresh their faith in the everlasting. Clergy who need to tell stories about themselves are similar to therapists who do the same. They are uncertain of their relationship with the "others" who come to them, and they want to bridge the gap by being a "regular person." It doesn't work that way.

Religion professionals typically think of people's faith as intellectual and consequently try to interact with them at that level. For most people, faith and religious practice are primarily intellectually driven, but there are also believers and regular church goers who respond to religion largely on an emotional plane. They may have very little foundation in the teachings of the denomination and little interest in being better informed. Theirs is a more personal and direct connection with the deity and often includes various parent images. Their contact with the Almighty is usually frequent and often volatile as God shares their anger, their sadness, their anxieties, and their joys. They experience religious services, including homilies, on a feeling level, and the impact on their spiritual life depends on the affective power of the liturgy. Their faith is neither transitory nor irresolute, but it is capricious. Unfortunately scholarly and intellectually focused clergy have difficulty understanding, communicating with, or relating to them.

Let us look at the other side of the fence where the therapist resides and deals with people of various religious beliefs. There is clearly an increased interest in this aspect of counseling evidenced by the patients who seek a "Christian counselor" and the popularity of graduate schools for pastoral counselors. The director of the Graduate Program in Pastoral Counseling at Loyola College in Maryland recently told me that applications to the program continue to grow each year. Some of the increase is related to new students from evangelical denominations. Will this new emphasis tend to divide therapists into two groups and create a sense of alienation between the "born-again Christians" and other believers? Or will the presence of this new group encourage all therapists to be more alert to religious issues and faith concerns?

The Diagnostic and Statistical Manual of Mental Disorders (DSM-IV) (American Psychiatric Association, Washington, D.C. 1994) contains a section relating to "Other Conditions That May Be a Focus of Clinical Attention." That section includes "Religious or Spiritual Problem" and gives as examples, "distressing experiences that involve loss or questioning of faith, problems associated with conversion to a new faith, or questioning of spiritual values that may not necessarily be related to an organized church or religious institution." DSM-IV is generally accepted in all teaching institutions and should, therefore, be familiar to all trained and licensed therapists. It would be unfortunate if those designated as Christian counselors or as pastoral counselors made assumptions that those not similarly trained might be limited in confronting the "Religious or Spiritual Problems" of their patients. It would also be divisive if those in need of counseling were encouraged by religion professionals to seek help exclusively from "Christian" therapists. If one is looking for therapy, it is better to see a good therapist who may be an atheist than a poor therapist who is a devout believer.

I recently had occasion in the classroom to present a situation in which a woman who had been in therapy for several weeks expressed her decision to obtain a divorce. The students were asked how they would proceed. A student replied that she felt it was her responsibility to preserve the marriage bond and would respond accordingly. Counselors must recognize that they are in a position to exercise exceptional influence over a patient, and that is precisely why they have an ethical obligation to observe neutrality and permit the patient to make the choices. A more appropriate therapeutic response would have been to encourage the woman to elaborate on her decision and to review thoughtfully and thoroughly her reasoning and, of course, to ask her about how this fit in with the teaching of her church and with her own spirituality. If the therapist does not have information about the woman's faith or spirituality, this would be a suitable time to ask about it. Based on the position espoused so definitely by the student, it seemed clear that her opposition to divorce was based solely on her religious beliefs and had no connection to any religious belief or practice of the patient. In the book previously quoted, Elie Wiesel wrote, "Every human being is a sanctuary, for God resides there. And nobody has the right to violate it." I believe that includes counselors.

Religious patients often speak of wanting to know God's will in relation to some decision they are about to make. It is important to go slowly in responding. Some patients believe they discover God's will in personal signs which seem to be known only to them. If a patient says to a therapist "I am changing jobs because I know God wants me to" or "It has become clear to me that divorcing my spouse would be acceptable to God," it would certainly be appropriate to ask lots of questions about how the decision came about without questioning the decision. Most religious people have at some time made a certain decision in life which they felt had been influenced by something beyond the known, something mystical. We must respect the mystery in our patients' lives. On the other hand, if a patient talks in a more open way about wanting to know God's will I sometimes suggest that God gave us tools to use in working at life. Among other personal assets, our tool box includes intelligence and emotions, and I believe God meant us to use them in evaluating what we are about to do as well as what we have done.

In considering mental health and spirituality it is important to maintain distinctions between them. Spiritually oriented therapists sometimes take the position that emotional disabilities limit a person's virtue. In the era after World War II several French scholars took up this question and produced a number of essays on the subject. Many of these were published in the book, "Cross Currents of Psychiatry and Catholic Morality" edited by William Birmingham and Joseph E. Cunneen (Pantheon Books, New

York, 1964). In a chapter by Piet Fransen there is the following comment, "It would also be a mistake to think that only the normal, balanced, psychically sane and 'integral' man, and even then only the man who observes the norms of Christian morality, can be reached by grace."

There is also a beautiful passage in the chapter by Louis Beirnaert: "There are the saints whose psychic structures are deformed and difficult, the company of the anguished, aggressive and sensual, all those who bear an insupportable weight of determinisms: the failures in whose heart there will always be a 'viper's tangle', the unfortunate, because they are born with a 'harelip." Therapists must be careful not to play God in making judgments or in trying to determine which course of action is the one a patient should take. Among the saints, Beirnaert finds those "with a psychic structure haunted by monsters" and those "with a psychic structure visited by angels." One of my God-images is that of the Master Psychiatrist who really does know **everything** about the person to be judged. To me that is a consoling thought. I mentioned in an earlier chapter telling students that if they find they don't like a patient, all they have to do is continue to discover more and more about the person, and they will eventually feel differently.

Statements in this chapter and in others have indicated that therapists should maintain neutral and accepting attitudes toward patients and in no way try to influence their choices but support self-determination. One can certainly raise the question, "How realistic are these recommendations?" People do influence one another in countless and continuing ways. Therapists are no exception. The therapist's temperament, personality, demeanor, and attitudes about life may be a prominent part of the treatment relationship for some patients. Many of those who come for help are there because they have an enhanced sensitivity to the feelings and the unspoken reactions of others. They surely do not discard their antennae when they come into the office.

So the therapist must acknowledge that the kind of person he or she is will be communicated in some way to the patient. Can you imagine spending hours and hours with someone and coming away not feeling that you know a lot about the person just from your observations? I do not believe that therapists "establish rapport" with a patient by talking about their own lives. Neither do they build the relationship by expressed interest or apparent concern. They create a therapeutic bond by genuine attention and sincere respect which, when we get right down to it, probably means that the therapist cannot be as neutral as we have suggested earlier. I don't believe I've ever seen a patient about whom I felt neutral. We need to distinguish between feeling engaged and supportive and caring, on the one hand, and acting in a biased manner, on the other.

Most people have had the benefit of good parents, good friends, and good neighbors. There are other individuals who have not been blessed with these positive experiences either in their childhood or in their adult life. If we ask them how they filled this void in their life, we usually find that one or possibly two individuals reached out in some way and gave them a feeling of being special, of being worthwhile. "Aunt Mary always seemed really interested in what I was doing." "My friend never seemed to get tired of listening to my woes when I was young." "My sixth grade teacher believed in me." "Whatever I did I knew my grandfather would always forgive me." "My friend, Julie, always thought I was the greatest." "The woman next door always smiled and said how glad she was to see me." "My high school science teacher had a way of making me feel better about myself, important." There is "a spirit of goodness" in some people to which we respond. Although it is not a necessary ingredient of treatment, therapists often impart this feeling to the patients they see. This is not the exclusive domain of therapists who practice a religion or follow a specific belief. It appears when we are aware of the dignity of each person and awed by the mystery that is present.

On September 12, 2006, an article in the Washington Post by Michelle Boorstein gave a report of a survey on religion from Baylor University, a leading Baptist institution. Among several interesting results, there were data relating to different views of the Deity. God was seen as authoritarian by 31.4% of the respondents, distant by 24.4%, benevolent by 23.0% and critical by 16.0%. It seems that God did not fair too well with people. It makes me wonder why families, friends, or neighbors never sufficiently impressed these respondents with goodness and love and generosity to give them a sense of a benevolent Supreme Being. On the other hand, people may lose the vision of divine bounty and goodness because they are so overwhelmed by the harsh events in their own lives or engulfed by the daily death and destruction that confronts us all. Patients are searching for faith in themselves when they come for therapy. In the process they may reestablish faith in others and faith in a power beyond their vision.

There are numerous books written about the care of "caregivers," indicating that those who take care of others may be detrimentally influenced by their work. Certainly therapists cannot deny that they are affected by the patients with whom they meet. It seems appropriate to close this last chapter with some comments about the influence that patients have on those who care for them. Treatment professionals should feel privileged to know the many remarkable people who are willing to share their struggles, their heart aches, their sadness, their humor, their courage, and, at times, their triumphs with their therapists. We mourn the tragedies of their lives; we find bravery in their continuing to push forward; we rejoice in their successes; and we recognize in them a strength of spirit which we sometimes wish we could make our own. The patients whom I have discussed in this book were presented to aid the reader in understanding the vagaries of emotional life and the victories of the human psyche.

In coming for therapy each new patient opens a book of life which we proceed to read together, carefully and reverentially. The reading should not be an embarrassment for the patient or a burden for the therapist. It is my hope that those who read this book will come to understand and appreciate the powerful emotional forces that exist within them and that they will use that energy to enrich their own lives and the lives of others with the love, the compassion, and the kindness that all religions preach.

www.ingramcontent.com/pod-product-compliance
Lightning Source LLC
Chambersburg PA
CBHW020426290526
45784CB00012BA/393